THE
HIDDEN
LEADER

THE
HIDDEN
LEADER

Discover and Develop Greatness

Within Your Company

SCOTT K. EDINGER · LAURIE SAIN

**Foreword by James M. Kouzes
and Barry Z. Posner**

AMERICAN MANAGEMENT ASSOCIATION

New York • Atlanta • Brussels • Chicago • Mexico City • San Francisco
Shanghai • Tokyo • Toronto • Washington, D.C.

Bulk discounts available. For details visit:
www.amacombooks.org/go/specialsales
Or contact special sales:
Phone: 800-250-5308
Email: specialsls@amanet.org
View all the AMACOM titles at: www.amacombooks.org

Library of Congress Cataloging-in-Publication Data
Edinger, Scott K.
  The hidden leader : discover and develop greatness within your company / Scott K. Edinger, Laurie Sain.
       pages cm
  Includes bibliographical references and index.
  ISBN 978-0-8144-3399-7 (hardcover) — ISBN 0-8144-3399-5 (hardcover) —
  ISBN 978-0-8144-3400-0 (ebook) 1. Leadership. 2. Employee motivation.
3. Corporate culture. I. Sain, Laurie. II. Title.
  HD57.7.E325 2014
  658.4'092--dc23
                        2014026448

About AMA

American Management Association (www.amanet.org) is a world leader in talent development, advancing the skills of individuals to drive business success. Our mission is to support the goals of individuals and organizations through a complete range of products and services, including classroom and virtual seminars, webcasts, webinars, podcasts, conferences, corporate and government solutions, business books, and research. AMA's approach to improving performance combines experiential learning—learning through doing—with opportunities for ongoing professional growth at every step of one's career journey.

Printing Number

10   9   8   7   6   5   4   3   2   1

To hidden leaders everywhere.
You are the powerhouses driving creativity,
productivity, and innovation in business.

Contents

List of Tools

As you read *The Hidden Leader*, you will find the worksheets and assessments in an order that helps you understand the concepts and ideas in the book. In the appendix, the tools are organized into a succinct process that you can use to evaluate hidden leaders and your organization. See the introduction to the appendix for more information.

Foreword

Leaders are everywhere we look. For more than three decades, we've been traveling the world constantly researching the practices of exemplary leadership and the qualities people look for and admire in leaders they would willingly follow. We've talked to people from every type of organization, public and private, government and nongovernment, high tech and low tech, small and large, schools and professional services. They are young and old, male and female, and from every ethnic group. They represent every imaginable vocation and avocation. They reside in every country we've studied. And they all have a story to tell.

Conventional wisdom portrays leadership as if it were found mostly at the top. Myth and legend have treated leadership as if it were the private reserve of a very few charismatic men and women. Nothing is further from the truth. We have examined the immense variety of stories from so many different people and places, and it has become crystal clear to us that leadership is not a gene. It's not a birthright. Demographics play no role in whether or not someone is going to become an exemplary leader. It's not about position or title. It's not about power or authority. It's not about being a CEO, president, general, or prime minister. Leadership is not about *who* you are or *where* you come from. It's about *what* you do. Our images of who's a leader and who's not are all mixed up in our preconceived notions about what leadership is and isn't.

Scott and Laurie are right on target when they say any organization that can harness the leadership talent of all of its employees has a competitive advantage. By shining a light on the "hidden" leaders—those individuals who act like leaders, regardless of their position or job description—they call our attention to what it takes to discover, nurture, and support the leadership talents within each person—talents that, while they may be hidden, are actually abundant in every organization.

Our multinational and cross-generational data, along with theirs, challenge the myth that leadership is about position and power. And those data support the fact that leadership is about the actions you take. One individual in Asia told us it became very clear to her, when she reflected on her personal-best leadership experience, "that leadership is everywhere, it takes place every day, and leadership can come from anyone. It doesn't matter that you don't have the title of 'manager,' 'director,' 'CEO' to go with it. In the end, that's all they are—titles on business cards and company directories. Being a true leader transcends all that."

Another individual contributor, from the United States, recognized that growing up, she had "assumed leaders had certain traits and qualities that I didn't seem to have. I thought there were 'natural' leaders who were born to lead. I thought leadership was the description of what these people did." Upon reflection she realized, "to my surprise, that I had those leadership traits." Hidden leaders are those people in your organization who share the belief that what they do matters, that their project, team, or organization would be less successful if it weren't for their efforts. These feelings translate into not only the additional discretionary effort they put into their work but also the leadership they are willing to exert to make extraordinary things happen.

Scott and Laurie have provided us with lots of concrete ideas about how positional leaders can identify and support the people in their organization who are, and could be, providing leadership. Their experiences, along with our data, clearly show that in the best organizations, everyone, regardless of title or position, is encouraged to act as a leader. That's because in these places people don't just believe that everyone can make a difference; they act in ways to develop and grow people's leadership talents. Scott and Laurie want this to be true of your organization.

Joon Chin Fum-Ko, director of people development and engagement at Infocomm Development Authority of Singapore, describes that thinking and action as "working to build an organization and culture where everyone feels that they are leaders, regardless of what they do, and appreciates that what each one of us does has an impact." Scott and Laurie provide many strategies and tools for doing just this. On a number of occasions they show how we can make some simple shifts in our thinking to leverage great results. Consider, for example, what it means if "the end defines the means," or what would be different if the organization was "customer purposed" rather than customer driven, or measurement systems were used "to improve, rather than prove"?

What you should also appreciate about this book is its scale. You don't have to be in the C-suite to take advantage of their advice and perspective. Indeed, you really don't even need to be in a position of leadership to learn about becoming an even more effective leader. After all, as one of our MBA students summed up in his concluding essay for our leadership course:

"Where do I start becoming a better leader? This question has been nagging me for some time. Naively I assumed that to become a better leader meant to perform formidable tasks: moving mountains, saving lives, changing the world for the better. Then it occurred to me—I was thinking selfishly. What I envisioned was instant gratification, recognition for my skills and talent. I found that every day I had an opportunity to make a small difference. I could have coached someone better, I could have listened better, I could have been more positive toward people, I could have said 'Thank you' more often, I could have . . . the list just went on. At first, I was a bit overwhelmed with the discovery of how many opportunities I had in a single day to act as a better leader. But as I have gotten to put these ideas into practice I have been pleasantly surprised by how much improvement I have been able to make by being more conscientious and intentional about acting as a leader."

That's the point for all of us—those of us in formal positions of leadership, those acting as "hidden" leaders, those emerging as leaders, and those aspiring to simply make the world a better place. Each day provides countless chances to make a difference. The chance might come in a private conversation with a direct report or in a meeting with colleagues. It might come over the family dinner table. It might come when you're speaking at a conference on the future of some new technology or methodology, or it might come when you're listening to a friend talk about a current conflict with a peer. There are countless leadership moments each day, and many moments each day when you can choose to make it possible for others to lead.

That's the secret Scott and Laurie are trying to share in this book: As they say in the epilogue, "Someone's contribution to the value of a business need not be constrained by that person's position on the organizational chart." Well said. Now put this idea into practice. Read on.

—James M. Kouzes and Barry Z. Posner
Coauthors, *The Leadership Challenge: How to Make Extraordinary Things Happen in Organizations* and *The Truth About Leadership: The No-Fads, Heart-of-the-Matter Facts You Need to Know*

THE
HIDDEN
LEADER

How to Use This Book

The *Hidden Leader* contains access to online resources that are integrated into the content. Worksheets and analytical tools in the book are available via your smartphone, tablet, or computer.

As you read, you'll see what are commonly called quick response, or QR, codes printed on pages with worksheets or other resources. Near the code will be a short url, or web address, that will access the same information. The codes and url resemble the ones in Figure I-1.

Figure I-1: Typical QR (quick response) code and its related short url.

bit.ly/19ruRwq

To use the QR codes, search for any QR code reader on the web or in your app store. Once you download it to your smartphone or pad, you'll be able to read all of the codes in this book. Scan the QR codes by opening the app and focusing on the code. Your phone will take you automatically to the resource you want.

To use the short urls, simply type in the address on your smartphone, tablet, or computer, using your usual web browser. You'll get directly to the resource on *The Hidden Leader* website at www.thehiddenleader.com.

While on the website, look around and see what else is available to help you use the information in the book. Join the *Hidden Leader* community to connect with others interested in developing greatness within their company.

Welcome to *The Hidden Leader*—the interactive book about leadership!

What Is a Hidden Leader?

Hidden leaders are all around you within your organization. You have worked with them, encouraged them, and seen them rise within organizations to positions of power and influence. You may have been a hidden leader early in your career.

You and others have called these workers smart, crucial, effective, or an important part of the company. You have seen them work effectively with people at many levels within the organization, from front lines to executive suites, regardless of their formal positions. But if you thought at all about these employees' abilities, you probably categorized them as having natural talent that couldn't be replicated. You didn't see them as leaders.

We believe differently. We believe these hidden leaders are a source of great strategic advantage in your company. They can be defined, identified, nurtured, and encouraged to help an organization develop a competitive edge. Some of these leaders will move up the organizational chart, accepting positional power as their personal influence and power develop. Others will prefer to stay at a certain level in the organization and bring their personal influence to bear on the work they love to do. As modern organizations develop new structures, both flat and virtual, we believe it is important to know how to spot and encourage hidden leaders and bring their abilities to bear on the toughest challenges in an organization. We also believe focusing on the skills and characteristics of hidden leaders can make all your employees more productive and satisfied.

Hidden leaders are not invisible to the people around them. What makes them "hidden" is not that their coworkers and supervisors do not value them as important players within the company. It is that management does not think of them as leaders with the potential to drive excellence throughout the organization.

Many people define leaders as people high up within management ranks or those likely to be tapped as future managers and executives. This definition implies that leadership flows downhill from those in acknowledged high positions. It also positions leaders as somewhat above the everyday challenges that characterize frontline responsibilities.

Our definition of hidden leaders is that they are the powerhouses within organizations who help galvanize people toward excellence. Generally, hidden leaders have little or no positional power. They are in frontline jobs or possibly lower-level supervisory positions. They may not be viewed as people likely to take on managerial responsibilities. Their leadership is disconnected from the traditional positional power of supervisors, managers, and executives. This disconnect does not undermine their leadership; it simply hides them from those with more traditional views of leadership.

Hidden leaders guide people's decisions on many levels of an organization. They are the origin of the upflow of leadership. This grassroots leadership is powerful because it emerges from people on the front lines who see the daily impact of executive decisions on products, processes, customers, and stakeholders. By leading from lower in the hierarchy, hidden leaders provide new insights to executives and official leaders who no longer experience frontline challenges.

The power of hidden leaders is obvious to those around them. These top individual contributors are known as the ones to approach for tough problems, the people new hires are directed to meet to understand the company's inner workings, and the anchors of productivity, creativity, and innovation.

We propose that hidden leaders are not just great workers: They are leaders in their own right. Managers who identify and treat them as leaders gain an important strategic and competitive advantage over the competition.

Hidden leaders provide the underlying energy that drives organizations forward, in our estimation. It's the hidden leaders throughout an organization who galvanize others to do their best work. They might become team leaders when a company depends on cross-functional teams to develop products or services. Where organizational charts flatten, hidden leaders create cores of productivity and help others get what they need to succeed. Hidden leaders are truly hidden in virtual organizations, especially short-term ones where people are working at a physical distance from one another and must find ways to be productive as a unit in spite of it.

Identifying hidden leaders isn't just about finding people who can become supervisors and managers or fulfill an organization's succession planning. Not all hidden leaders will want to move up the organization, nor should you expect to be able to promote each one.

As a manager, the better you can uncover the hidden leaders within your organization, the more you can encourage, develop, and promote them and their work. Hidden leaders can become a core strategic and competitive advantage for a company. Cadres of hidden leaders free managers and executives to focus on the organization's cutting-edge challenges. They become de facto supervisors in small groups or teams because others look to them for advice or help. Hidden leaders are also courageous enough to speak the truth to management, which usually leads to uncovering and solving problems below the radar of everyday actions.

Hidden leaders bring a company's value promise to life in ways no competitor can identify or match. These leaders do not appear on the organizational chart. They don't stand out on a company's roster with any specific, role-based characteristics. Their influence on innovations and processes is invisible to an outsider. This makes hidden leaders one of your most important competitive advantages. No one else can see them, much less replicate their influence. Hidden leaders address all three areas of innovation, process, and customer intimacy naturally.

Unfortunately, hidden leaders can be driven out of an organization if it punishes them for their very talents and skills. A wise supervisor or manager will notice what happens to an organization's hidden leaders. There may be cultural mismatches, signals of upcoming disasters, or evidence of a falling market share in the way a company treats its hidden leadership.

Hidden leaders affect the bottom line of an organization in several ways. They strive to fulfill the company's value promise; they enable effective shortcuts to be devised without sacrificing quality; they inspire others around them to do their best work. When the time comes to find potential supervisors and managers, of course, being able to spot and develop hidden leaders is crucial. But when such succession is not at issue, hidden leaders positively influence the energy of an organization, which can result in more creativity, productivity, and profit.

CHAPTER ONE

The Dynamics of Hidden Leadership

You will see hidden leaders in different phases of their development in your organization. Some will be fully developed; others will need some skill development or a nudge in the right direction to become more capable.

Before you can identify and develop hidden leaders, it's important to know what hidden leadership is. The dynamics of hidden leadership are more than effectiveness, friendliness, and productivity. They encompass specific facets of behavior and attitude that result in these leaders fulfilling the value promise of your organization.

As we've said, these leaders are well known within your organization but usually not seen as leaders per se by their supervisors and managers. This chapter helps you understand what hidden leaders are so you can begin to discover them in your organization.

To discover and develop a hidden leader, a manager must know how to identify the leader through actions and results. In our experience with hundreds of companies and thousands of leaders, these actions spring from a unique dynamic. It begins when hidden leaders demonstrate integrity consistently, even in difficult situations. Beyond integrity—the sine qua non of hidden leadership—these leaders lead others through authentic relationships, focus actions and processes on desired results, and remain highly customer purposed, even when they do not connect with paying customers regularly.

As a result of these four facets of hidden leadership, these leaders fulfill the value promise of the organization in everything they do. Hidden leaders understand the vision and intent of the value promise and evaluate their actions based on that promise. Fulfilling the value promise is sometimes seen as a characteristic in and of itself. It can look like "talent" or "drive" or "effectiveness," the words one might use to unknowingly describe hidden leaders. It is what enables hidden leaders to move from position to position or from company to company and maintain their hidden leadership abilities. They, and the people they influence, transcend the localized interests of job, peers, or department. It is this fulfillment of an organization's true value to its customers that makes hidden leaders such a powerful competitive advantage in the marketplace.

THE END RESULT: FULFILLING THE VALUE PROMISE

A successful organization promises something of value to its customers. The nature of the customer, and the customer's perceptions, dictates what that value is. Nonprofits promise change to their donors who want to influence the world. For-profit public companies promise earnings and growth to their shareholders by selling something of value to users. Even governments promise value—from protection to services.

But organizations often must consider other stakeholder demands that diverge wildly. Stockholders, for example, may want quarterly earnings and growth, which may conflict with paying customers' needs for an affordable, specific solution, and the board of directors' demands for innovation from R&D. How do organizations reconcile these sometimes conflicting demands for value from their stakeholders?

In our view, the definition of the value promise of an organization is not simply the value that a specific stakeholder wants from an organization. The value promise is the fundamental production of value that is demanded by the customer who is indispensable—the one who pays the bills.

The value promise is rarely a product or service, because products and services are symptoms of the value that paying customers want. For example, electric utilities do not simply sell electricity. If electricity were what they sold, most customers would evaporate, because what can one do

Figure 1-1: The value promise is the sum total of benefits that paying customers receive from an organization.

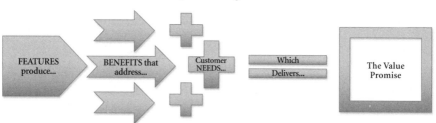

with a simple flow of electrons? Electric companies sell a convenient way for end-user customers to turn on their lights, heat their buildings, and run their computers, washing machines, and vacuum cleaners.

Seen in that light, the value promise of a utility company can be provided in many ways beyond the simple production and delivery of electricity. Yet providing that convenience is ultimately the value promise of the electric company: an affordable, convenient, and consistent way to keep our lights on, along with all of our other devices that depend on electric power.

We define the value promise as the benefit that paying customers receive from an organization's efforts. As sales professionals know, the value promise is completely different from customer needs, features, or benefits (see Figure 1-1).

- **Needs** are what customers acknowledge as something they want. In our utility example, the customer need is to be able to affordably use electrical devices without thinking about it beyond flipping a switch. Customer needs are often the linchpin of a company's efforts, but as Apple has shown, it's not the customers' responsibility to know what all their needs are.

- **Features** are the characteristics of a product or service that are instrumental to addressing the customers' needs—or, in the case of Apple, for providing an unexpected and cool experience. This is where many organizations get caught in thinking about what they sell. For electric utilities, features are power plants, power lines, outlets, wiring, and switches, all the physical elements that help keep the lights on.

- **Benefits** are the positive experience or economic value that customers receive for doing business with a company through its products and services. Let's face it: We don't need more wiring in our lives. But who among those of us with electricity doesn't want two things from our electric utility: not having to think about power and getting it to our homes by flipping a switch, all at an affordable cost? At the same time, the earnings that electric company stockholders receive are also benefits, albeit of a very different nature than those of the consumer. The benefits for employees because of all of this activity are reliable, consistent jobs within a culture that matches their personal cultural needs.
- **The value promise** goes one step beyond benefits. The value promise is the sum total of benefits that are valuable to the customer who pays the bills. Essentially, the value promise is met in the mind of the customer not by a specific feature or benefit. This customer may or may not be the end user. For example, for nonprofits, the customers who pay the bills are the donors. Meeting those people's needs is sometimes more important than addressing the social ills to which the nonprofit is devoted, because without donors the desired social change will not occur. (This explains many universities' propensity to run extravagant football programs to support educational ones, because alumni who donate money to their alma maters tend to love a winning football team.) For utilities, the value promise is the convenience and affordability of keeping the lights on for the paying customer—in this case, the end user. Stockholders are a part of the equation, but without paying customers, utilities would be hard pressed to provide any value to people who own their stock.

This definition of a value promise seems intuitive, but we see many companies, and some whole industries, that are confused about who pays the bills. Some insurance companies, for example, seem to forget who provides the money they use to invest and settle claims. Collecting money from customers and making it difficult for them to receive compensation for valid claims in order to please stockholders with more earnings is not an indication that the company understands what a value promise is, yet we often hear horror stories about insurance companies that appear to do just that.

There are, of course, insurance companies that are reasonable and honorable when it comes to claims. In 2008, the one-hundred-year-old historic wooden building in Lander, Wyoming, where Laurie had had her office for fifteen years, burned to the ground through no fault of her own. Within hours of the fire's start, Laurie's local State Farm insurance agent, Leslie Calkins, called her to say she had begun the claims process (the fire wasn't nearly out yet). Within days, State Farm sent Laurie a check for part of her total claim amount while she worked through the shock of losing thirty years' worth of work and art and began a list of items she could remember. Over the course of a year, the company helped Laurie create her list and calculate a value for her lost stuff, and paid without question up to the amount of Laurie's insurance.

State Farm's response made dealing with a business catastrophe as easy as could be expected. It also made Laurie a State Farm customer for life—for her vehicles, home, rentals, and office. She's also sort of become a walking ad for the company among her friends and acquaintances (and now readers). This long-term loyalty will lead to State Farm recouping at least part of its claim costs throughout Laurie's (hopefully long) lifetime.

State Farm knows what its value promise is: to help its paying customers cope with financially devastating events without having to fight for support. That is the value that drives the company's success and helps it meet all other stakeholder needs—including those of investors and employees.

As we looked at the hidden leaders we have experienced over thirty years, we discovered that the most obvious characteristic of hidden leaders is that they consistently and courageously act out the value promises of their organizations. We see this commitment to the value promise with existing and potential paying customers. Hidden leaders may not be able to articulate it, but they clearly understand at a gut level what it is that drives the organization's success. But these actions don't happen automatically. Let's investigate closely the dynamics of hidden leadership, which begins with demonstrated integrity and results in these leaders acting out the value promise consistently.

THE FOUR FACETS OF HIDDEN LEADERSHIP

Hidden leaders clearly display four facets in their behaviors and results: they demonstrate integrity, lead through relationships, focus on results, and remain customer purposed whether or not they work directly with paying customers.

The fundamental characteristic that enables hidden leadership to bloom is *demonstrating integrity*. Sometimes that integrity means taking a stance that is not immediately lucrative, helpful, or easy to discuss. But it is held because the hidden leader is committed to her integrity.

For the hidden leaders we have seen in action, visible integrity isn't an optional stance. It is the foundation of their being, of feelings of self-worth and satisfaction. We believe that demonstrating integrity is indispensable for hidden leaders. Through it, they clarify their other critical skills. While many hidden leaders can work within companies and cultures that don't support these other skills, few will remain where their integrity is either dismissed as irrelevant or made impossible to express.

Leading through relationships enables the hidden leader to build trust and a strong base of people who are influenced by and willing to help the hidden leader. It's the personal, or "people," aspect of hidden leadership and one that an effective leader needs no matter the position in a company.

Hidden leaders' relationships are authentic ones, where both parties value the connection. Hidden leaders are far from nice guys or manipulative, so-called friends. Hidden leaders truly like and strive to understand people and act in ways that benefit both whenever possible. If relationships involve conflict, which they inevitably do at some points, hidden leaders have skills than enable them to work through potential land mines and deepen the relationship for both people.

Focusing on results is the process aspect of hidden leadership. Hidden leaders who keep the end result foremost in their thoughts can adjust processes and procedures effectively. By focusing on results, hidden leaders evaluate their actions against the goals they want to achieve. For hidden leaders, the ends define the means, they don't justify the means. This critical difference results in hidden leaders' striving to meet the end goal and addressing conflicts or challenges with thoughtful, coherent actions.

Finally, hidden leaders are *customer purposed*. This facet animates the purpose aspect of hidden leadership. Determining how to address customer needs to benefit both customer and company makes actions purposeful and thus meaningful, and not just for the hidden leader. Because of the leader's relationships and the trust engendered by them, this purposeful enthusiasm spreads from the hidden leader to others. Individuals in the organization trust hidden leaders and, knowing their deep integrity, more easily embrace the same sense of purpose and meaning.

As a manager, you must understand each of these four facets in depth, including what drives them in hidden leaders and what undermines them in terms of systems or support. You will then be able to discover hidden leaders in your organization and develop them appropriately to strengthen your company's competitive opportunities.

Demonstrates Integrity

In the 1997 film *Grosse Point Blank*, John Cusack plays a hit man, troubled by his past, who describes himself as having a "certain . . . moral flexibility." As the audience, we laugh, because certainly someone who kills others for a living is nothing if not morally flexible.

But we laugh for another reason: Morals, and the actions we do according to them, can be flexible for most of us in many situations. We have each told a white lie to protect someone's feelings, or justified "borrowing" a pencil from work because it wasn't "really" stealing. Our morals are often codes of conduct that we adjust to demands of specific moments in our lives.

But if the film's writers had characterized Cusack's character as having a certain "flexibility of integrity," we would not have gotten the joke. Because integrity, by its definition, means adhering consistently to a strong, reliable code of ethics, whatever that code is. (It also, by the way, describes the sound structure of something, like the integrity of a boat's hull. That image reminds us of integrity's moral strength and importance as well.)

Note that integrity doesn't mean someone believes in and acts on the same moral or ethical code that we believe in. It means a person maintains a cohesive, strong, personal definition of what is right and wrong and consistently acts in accordance with those principles. Whether or not you as a manager agree with a hidden leader's principles is another matter. For example, some hidden leaders may have a much stronger sense of what is fair or honest than most people. That doesn't mean the hidden leader is somehow right and others are wrong. It does mean that the hidden leader is more likely to raise issues around those principles that others will have to consider.

Demonstrating integrity is the absolute bottom-line requirement of hidden leadership. In our experience, hidden leaders are known for their integrity and for acting on it in difficult situations where some might forgo commitments and lean on moral flexibility. But hidden leaders do not. Their integrity shows consistently along the way. An observer can identify it in actions, words, and attitudes.

We believe that to demonstrate integrity, a person must have the courage to consistently adhere to a strong ethical code, even in difficult situations (see Figure 1-2). Let's investigate that idea, beginning with the notion of a strong ethical code.

By "a strong ethical code," we mean more than simply not lying, cheating, or stealing. Those characteristics are the minimum expectations for any employee—the absence of outright dishonest behavior. A strong ethical code is built on positive, action-oriented, baseline beliefs that guide

Figure 1-2: The critical elements of demonstrating integrity.

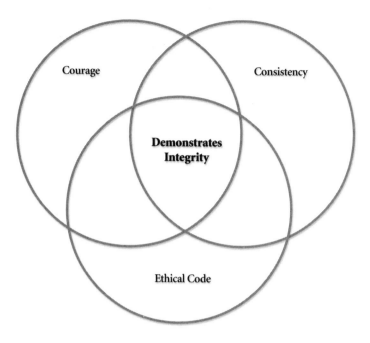

behavior. Hidden leaders may not be able to describe those beliefs, but others will see them consistently in action.

For example, one familiar baseline belief is the Greek concept of the Golden Rule: treating others as you would like others to treat you. Under this belief, stealing is wrong to a hidden leader because no one wants to fall victim to a thief.

Hidden leaders may hold many other baseline beliefs. Some may be based in religious tenets and ethics; others lean on more philosophical concepts such as the Golden Rule. However hidden leaders define their beliefs or underlying principles, they are focused on the welfare of everyone, not just the actor.

Hidden leaders are conscious of strong definitions of right and wrong that transcend specific moments. The hidden leader's ethical code is broad enough to apply to all situations. The code determines present decisions based on the likely outcome or result of the leader's actions. In this sense, the hidden leader's ethics are linked to a focus on results. While a strong ethical code is not defined by the results of the actions—that would imply that the ends justify the means, which hidden leaders do not believe—the ethics do consider the benefits to everyone involved in the situation.

For example, a hidden leader with a strong ethical code may believe that telling the truth is central to good communication. When a colleague needs feedback to improve performance, the hidden leader will look for a situation when that colleague can best hear and handle the feedback. A hidden leader will not choose to give feedback to a colleague in a staff meeting when the feedback concerns the colleague alone. That feedback will be given privately, so the colleague is not embarrassed or harmed in the eyes of others by the leader's feedback.

On the other hand, asked in a staff meeting about a colleague's performance, the same hidden leader will find a way to say the truth. But the leader will do so in a way that benefits the colleague and staff without initiating unnecessary discord or conflict.

The hidden leader's ethical code embodies these two fundamental characteristics: Ethical principles apply to all situations (in other words, the hidden leader maintains ethical consistency), and the impact on the whole or the group affects how the leader fulfills those principles.

One common notion holds that ethics can be defined as what one does when no one is looking. Others may say ethics is what you do when you know you won't be caught. Given these definitions, many people's ethical codes would be very slim indeed.

Most of us like to think we are consistent in how we apply our ethics or morals to all situations, whether anyone is watching (or catching) us or not. At the least, most of us know what we should be doing or saying to remain consistent to our ideals.

Some people, however, do not apply their ethical values consistently. We have all known strong, intelligent, and capable people who are very ethical as long as they are acting in a public venue. Left alone or in a situation where no one can know their actions, these people often ignore their ethical codes and do whatever it takes to advance their careers, reputations, and finances.

In our experience, hidden leaders maintain ethical consistency in their actions, thoughts, and words, even though there may be no chance that anyone will ever know what it is they did. They are satisfied and perhaps proud of the things they privately do that benefit others or the group. Above all else, while they might be flexible in how they apply their ethical code, they are inflexible when it comes to adhering to it. We call this characteristic ethical consistency.

Being ethically consistent in all situations, in public or private, results in more of an impact than just remaining true to one's ethical ideals. It also means others can predict what hidden leaders will do. Consistency generates trust in the hidden leader's judgment and ethical codes. It equates to being dependable.

Because of ethical consistency, people know that hidden leaders will do what they say they will do, in the best manner possible. People also know that if a situation becomes difficult or dangerous, hidden leaders will be some of the first to raise the issue for discussion and resolution. Further, because people see hidden leaders applying ethical models consistently but in ways that benefit the people involved, they often turn to hidden leaders for advice on how they might act in specific situations.

For example, in one small company we worked in, a colleague approached one hidden leader about a supervisor's tendency to bad-mouth the company's customers to employees. This upset the colleague tremendously. She asked the hidden leader for advice. The hidden leader offered to present the issue anonymously to the supervisor. Emboldened by the support, the colleague asked if the hidden leader would accompany her to meet the supervisor and raise the issue in a discussion. The two brainstormed an approach that entailed pointing out the damage the supervisor's comments did to other employees' attitudes. The conversation with the supervisor was a success. The supervisor had not been thinking about the effect his comments had on employees; he had simply been letting off steam in a way that seemed safe because he trusted the people who worked for him. The issue was resolved without involving the supervisor's manager, and the supervisor became more aware of his impact on the people around him. The hidden leader's commitment to honest communication was the basis for the supervisor's change.

Hidden leaders' abilities to respond to others' requests for help lean on other facets of hidden leadership, including leading through relationships and focusing on results. However, it is hidden leaders' ethical consistency that builds the strongest foundation of trust. In one sense, this trust is at the core of hidden leadership itself. Ethical consistency translates into so many other important characteristics that without it a person would be hard-pressed to be any kind of a leader, much less a hidden leader.

Demonstrating ethical consistency means having courage to act in difficult situations. The ability to describe what is right is sometimes referred to as talking the talk. Hidden leaders who consistently apply their ethical codes can be described like this. There is more to integrity, however, than just knowing or describing the right thing to do. Integrity requires actually doing the right thing, even in situations that are difficult or ambiguous. This is sometimes known as walking the walk.

While we may argue that ethical consistency is the foundation of hidden leadership, courage is also critical to demonstrating integrity. Courage is similar to the initiative to act we describe as being part of a focus on results later in this chapter. But initiative describes taking advantage of a situation and acting to benefit everyone involved. Courage is required when situations are potentially toxic: when reputations, relationships, and futures might be at risk.

Hidden leaders look for alternative ways to consistently apply their ethics to meet challenging situations. They display the courage to do the right thing even when it is difficult. To say in a meeting, "This goes against our cultural values," or to tell a manager, "This policy does not mesh with our promise to put our customers first," requires deep courage. It demonstrates the ability to commit to an ethical code in all situations.

This courage is important, especially when an organization faces fundamental challenges to its business model, reputation, product development, or employee morale. Speaking the truth to people with positional power in the organization is difficult. Since, by definition, most hidden leaders are not yet in positions of power or management, they must find ways to tell the truth and the courage to do so in spite of potential repercussions.

By courage, we don't mean that a person who brashly contradicts a company's leadership or a team's conclusions is acting courageously. Courage, especially in hidden leaders, can be fairly quiet. It adjusts responses to the demands of a situation. People's feelings, beliefs, and contributions are definitely part of the situation.

For example, one hidden leader in a consulting company saw a project manager consistently push contributors beyond the clear procedures and parameters that had been set, in order to meet changing customer demands. She also heard similar complaints from contributors on other teams, with different project managers. The hidden leader went to the department head and pointed out the challenge without naming specific project managers. The leader also suggested a potential solution: Involve contributors in conversations with customers before committing to changes in scope. As a result, the department head began a process analysis for the entire department. The procedural changes improved productivity and profitability as well as customer satisfaction.

Hidden leaders with courage manage to raise important issues in ways that others can accept. They also don't let critical challenges drop if, in the immediate situation, no one else rises to meet the challenge.

In one meeting, we saw a hidden leader contend that how a software company implemented its "continuous improvement" approach was demoralizing programmers and quality testers. The company seemed to take the word *continuous* literally, and changes were uncontrolled. Contributors could not address everything and make fixed deadlines. The manager running the meeting mentioned that the issue wasn't the topic of that meeting. The leader asked that it be posted on a "parking lot" list and dealt with soon. At this second request, other colleagues in the meeting concurred that something had to be done because people were losing their creative impulses. The manager noted the issue, and it was dealt with separately.

How organizations react to the courage of hidden leaders to raise important issues says more about the organization than the hidden leader. We'll discuss this later in this book in more depth. But in our experience, in any situation, hidden leaders find the courage to say and do the right thing, although the potential results may include reassignments, rejection, demotions, or firings.

Leads Through Relationships

Demonstrating integrity is a sine qua non for hidden leaders. But they also lead through relationships, because those relationships are important to them personally.

Early in her career, Laurie was hired as an instructional designer at a growing firm. She was thrilled to get the job: The work was interesting, the pay good, and her new boss seemed a personable, positive leader. Laurie looked forward to learning a lot since her boss was a talented and energetic woman who had been in the business for decades.

Some months into her tenure there, Laurie was assigned an experimental project, one that would be the flagship of a new set of products for the company. One morning, her boss (we'll call her Janet) came to see how the project was progressing.

Laurie and Janet chatted comfortably, and Laurie sensed that the work she was doing was impressive. But Laurie had a problem: A co-worker in another department, on whose work she depended, was not meeting deadlines. The problem seemed to be priorities: The other worker's supervisor declared that Laurie's project was less important than ongoing work. Laurie was getting behind, and she asked her boss what to do.

Janet listened with concern and said she would talk to the supervisor to make sure deadlines were met. Then she sighed mightily. "Sometimes I wish people would just grow up!" she exclaimed.

Laurie was startled. She didn't know what to say.

Janet continued, oblivious to Laurie's troubled expression. "I've had trouble with that guy before. I think he's afraid I'll take his place or something. Like I would want to! It's the worst part of being a manager," said Janet. "Dealing with people who let their insecurities get in the way of the work. Frankly, I don't really care—I just want to see the work done!"

Janet changed the subject and ended by encouraging Laurie's good work. After she left, Laurie wondered if some of her own insecurities—or lack of advanced expertise—would ever draw her boss's ire like that. She resolved to keep quiet about issues in the future and see if she could resolve them herself.

Laurie liked her boss and thought Janet liked her. Now she wasn't so sure she mattered to Janet at all, except as someone who got things done.

Laurie's experience with her new boss illustrates the importance of relational leadership. When Laurie felt that Janet was truly interested in her, she wanted to contribute and do her best for the organization. But a simple comment destroyed Laurie's confidence that she truly mattered to her boss and, by extension, to the organization.

While Janet was capable in her field, she was not strong in creating and maintaining relationships. Essentially, leading through relationships requires an authentic, honest interest in others at many levels of an organization. This is evidenced and created by certain skills, attitudes, and characteristics. The result is a leader who develops real relationships throughout a company. These relationships enable hidden leaders to positively influence the organization while taking an interest in those around them.

Whether a hidden leader is in a position of authority or not, it is obvious to co-workers and colleagues that the hidden leader's relationships are the basis of that leadership. Not all people in leadership positions have this trait. Hidden leaders, whether in a position of authority or not, display this ability to lead through relationships, or what we call relational leadership.

Essentially, those who lead through relationships:

◻ Use interpersonal skills effectively

◻ Exercise a sense of curiosity

◻ Value others

◻ Believe in their own personal value to others, whether as a co-worker or as a friend

We'll discuss specific interpersonal skills later in this book. For now, let's delve further into the influence relationships bring to hidden leaders, no matter what their roles in an organization.

In the business world, two aspects of power are familiar in an organization: positional power and personal power. Effective leaders in management positions certainly have positional power, but they may also have personal power: the ability to influence others to perform.

When we think of hidden leaders, we tend to think of this dichotomy in a different way. We posit positional leadership—the official delineation as boss, supervisor, or manager by an organization's management—versus relational leadership. The differences are clear:

◻ The positional leader is someone who, in a hierarchical, official relationship defined by the organization, is responsible to manage others' performance. It can be unclear to others whether these positional leaders could influence anyone without the supportive trappings of the position. Sadly, not all positional leaders are relational leaders (see Figure 1-3).

◻ Relational leaders—which hidden leaders are—lead and inspire because of who they are and how they interact with others. Relational leaders are well liked. Essentially, they care about others no matter what their positions or roles in the organization. These relationships are the foundation of the relational leader's influence on others.

Figure 1-3: Effective organizations combine relational and positional leaders whenever possible. (Use the online tool to evaluate your company.)

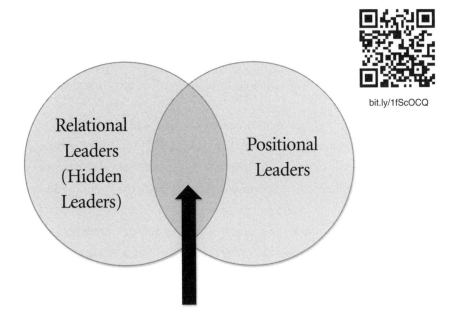

bit.ly/1fScOCQ

The relational leader operates not by being known by everyone, but by authentically creating positive relationships with people around her. Those people might be co-workers, teams, supervisors, or managers up to a company's C-level. A person who leads through relationships genuinely likes people for who they are, not for what they can do for that leader or the organization.

When we run workshops, we often ask participants to describe characteristics of the best and worst leaders they have worked with, whether or not those leaders held management positions. Then we ask them to compare the two sets of characteristics. A handful of common themes emerge.

One important distinction is that the best leaders maintain positive, quality relationships with people throughout the organization. They are relational leaders. This broad base helps leaders in several ways:

- ◘ When challenges arise, these leaders tap into the organization's creative talent to find a solution because they know who those talents are.

- Relational leaders influence others to do their best because the leaders themselves believe in the people around them.
- These leaders help individuals cope with specific challenges better because they value the human and emotional aspects of each person. They know that productivity depends as much on emotional strength and maturity as it does on knowledge, skill, and experience.

On the other hand, poor leaders are often described as manipulative, harsh, or demanding. They damage human relationships emotionally and professionally. Often, these are people in positional authority who do not like or trust their colleagues and act to maximize their reputations to those higher than them in the company hierarchy.

Poor positional leaders negatively affect morale, commitment, and engagement. People working under the pressure of a poor positional leader are doing the least amount of work possible without being fired. Needless to say, these positional leaders do not inspire commitment or creativity.

Not all positional leaders are poor leaders, of course. When relational leaders also hold positions of power, an organization benefits at all levels. Relational leaders enable creativity and innovation because they honestly value the people working within their company. That value means more to these leaders than productivity or success. It is based in an authentic regard for people in all roles within the organization.

Hidden leaders display the same characteristics as the best relational leaders in major organizations. They maintain a broad and, in some places, deep base of authentic relationships. They are neither a best friend to everyone lower than them in a hierarchy while ignoring management, nor a toady to supervisors and managers while ignoring everyone below them. Hidden leaders' relationships are concrete, authentic, and integrated into their personal identities.

Hidden leaders who lead through relationships may not know everyone, or the most important positional leaders in an organization. They do enjoy a wide range of positive relationships with people from all levels and areas in the organization. Importantly, they value the contributions of many areas, including those outside their own expertise.

One of Scott's projects was with a manufacturer of semiconductor equipment, a very technical organization on the front lines of engineering and manufacturing. The primary focus at all times was on the physical and technical aspects of the business, either the equipment that made its products or the final products themselves.

During one meeting, the group was heatedly discussing technical enhancements designed to create more product. Everyone's focus was on the engineering aspects of the company's machinery and potential R&D advances that could improve productivity overall.

As the conversation progressed, the productivity discussion stalled whenever a live person was identified as being involved in a step of the process. Suddenly, one of the team leads had an epiphany. "We should focus on our people and making them more productive," she said, "not just on the scientific side of our work. All of our products are produced with technical equipment, but most of our work is done by people."

This was a tectonic shift in how this organization viewed the work of its supervisors, who were highly precise and specialized. The team lead understood the power of leading through relationships. The ensuing conversation focused on improving levels of people's engagement throughout the team.

Focuses on Results

When Scott set up his new home office, he wanted it to reflect his new consulting company's identity. So his goal seemed simple: change his home telephone's caller ID from his wife's name to his own. One day when he had a few minutes to spare, he called his telephone company to make the change.

Two frustrating hours later, Scott sat with his wife and tried to calm himself with a glass of wine. He told her a little of what happened.

Perplexed, she asked, "What do you mean, we have to send back all of our Internet-related equipment?"

Scott felt himself getting angry all over again. "That's right. We have to cancel and disconnect all of our phone, cable, and Internet services for seventy-two hours, and mail our three HDTV boxes and router to the phone company so they can send the exact same equipment back to us. Then we pay a cancellation fee, pay a new start-up fee, and sign up as new customers!" He took a deep breath.

"All to change our caller ID? That makes no sense," said his wife.

"I guess being a loyal, paying customer for eleven years doesn't count for much anymore," fumed Scott. "The so-called customer service agent said she was 'just doing my job,' which was to manage customer connections and disconnections. Some kind of managing!"

Scott and his wife discussed their options. Perhaps it made sense to leave her name on the caller ID after all. But his wife finally persuaded Scott to call again, get a different service rep, and see if there was something else to be done. He agreed, reluctantly.

The next morning, anticipating at least one wasted hour, Scott called customer service and explained what he had been told the day before. The new agent listened, asked a few questions, and then helped Scott work through a different process that would change the caller ID within twenty-four hours. The agent would still have to charge Scott's account for the cancellation and start-up fees, but on her own initiative, she asked her supervisor to approve a credit equal to those two charges. Scott would end up paying nothing. He was astounded—and pleased. The entire conversation took less than twenty-five minutes.

Later that evening, he told the story to his wife.

"How was she able to do all that?" asked his wife.

"She said her job was to solve customers' problems," replied Scott. "Then she thanked me for being a loyal customer and made sure everything was ready to go."

"A new caller ID in twenty-four hours," mused his wife. "Now that's great customer service."

Scott's second experience with his phone company certainly illustrates great customer service. But what made the difference? Both agents he contacted had the same job, the same training, and the same pay scale. Both agents took actions to change Scott's caller ID on his phone. Yet one person approached the job as managing a fixed process; the other approached it as creating results for the customer.

You can probably guess which one we identify as a hidden leader: the second agent, who focused on results. The difference is clear. By focusing on results related to paying customers' needs, a hidden leader makes things happen for customers, co-workers, and the company.

When does a hidden leader focus on results? We believe it happens when the hidden leader maintains a wide perspective and acts with independent initiative. The result is individual engagement at a level that achieves more than knowledge, experience, or positive thinking alone. It entails using the end to define the means.

Hidden leaders maintain a broad perspective when it comes to aligning actions with goals. These goals are related to the company's value promise: Hidden leaders understand how their job responsibilities and actions fulfill the promise for the paying customer. Their goals reflect that understanding. Faced with complex decisions, hidden leaders' broad perspectives ensure that the end defines the means of getting the job done.

When the end defines the means, hidden leaders don't just do a job. They aim for the end they are supposed to produce—the goal. This goal usually benefits both the customer and the company. It doesn't depend on the established process, the status quo, or the personal needs of the leader.

By allowing the end to define the means to reach it, hidden leaders evaluate potential actions against the goal of the job. They balance the needs of the paying customer with established processes and procedures. Responses, decisions, and process steps are all measured and adjusted to ensure the goal is reached. If an action doesn't drive the hidden leader toward the goal, it isn't taken. Instead, other actions are identified or devised so they do move the leader closer to reaching the goal. The goal is the measure of what can be done, and what should be done, to reach it.

Hidden leaders know that procedures were developed to make tasks easier and more predictable, but that no process can address every situation for every customer. They do not let immediate concerns or crises dictate how the job should be done. They follow procedures but are willing to seek ways to adjust them when the broader perspective warrants it. Maintaining this long-term, larger perspective enables them to keep the goal—the ends—in sight and use it to determine the best actions to take to address the immediate customer need or situation.

By the way, "the end defines the means" doesn't imply an absence of process (see Figure 1-4). Process, especially in a large organization, is an important way to organize, manage, and audit performance in a company. However, when the end defines the means, the hidden leader questions and prioritizes process steps and procedures, and evaluates if or how those procedures will get the customer closer to the goal. Hidden leaders understand how to balance strict process against the needs of the customer. The leader then creates new, changed, or additional process steps and exceptions to reach the goal. With this approach, a hidden leader tips the scale in favor of results whenever possible.

Figure 1-4: The end defines the means when hidden leaders
balance customer needs and strict internal processes.

The Result of a Broad Perspective

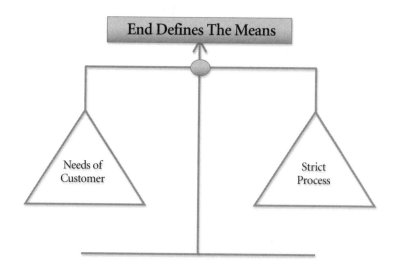

For example, Scott's second service agent could not avoid the automated cancellation and start-up fees, but she took the initiative to get a supervisor's permission to credit Scott's account with the same amount. She balanced the customer's desire for a new caller ID against the process and actually added a process step to ensure that a loyal customer would not be charged for what was, from the customer's point of view, a simple request. By checking in with her supervisor, she also ensured that her judgment of the situation was appropriate for the company and her solution was within the bounds of the company's needs.

Her initiative links to the second part of our definition of a focus on results: an independent initiative to act.

When the end defines the means, hidden leaders look for goal-directed actions that will help them achieve the results they want for their customer and their company. But just identifying those actions isn't enough. Someone has to act.

Typically, hidden leaders take personal initiative to complete actions without asking permission first from someone perceived as being in authority. Hidden leaders see themselves as having the authority themselves to make decisions and complete actions to reach goals. They feel responsible and accountable, not just for the demands of their jobs but also for successful outcomes for stakeholders involved. They see their roles broadly. They are not confined by specific procedures and job descriptions; they see themselves in terms of responsibilities and results.

At the same time, hidden leaders know where the boundaries are for themselves and their customers. If necessary, they will stretch a process to achieve a goal without breaking down the fundamental structures that support an organized workplace. They do this most effectively when, within the organization, ethical boundaries and organizational standards are clearly defined.

An independent initiative to act is similar to integrity's courage to act, but there is a subtle difference. In focusing on results, the hidden leader doesn't wait for permission. As a person with integrity, the hidden leader finds the courage to act when conflict is already in place. Initiative is the source of new solutions and innovations; courage is a means of halting progress down a wrong road. Both are important to the hidden leader's ability to be effective.

Remember Scott's second interaction with the phone company: The customer service rep explained that she could not alter the computer system that was going to charge him disconnect and start-up service fees. However, she did create an alternative—permission from her supervisor to credit Scott's account for the same amount. The end result was no financial impact on Scott. As a hidden leader, she stretched the boundaries of the existing process and found an alternative that achieved the goal and was minimally disruptive to the customer. Most important, she took this initiative on her own. She challenged established standards and process steps, deliberately and consciously, to reach the goal.

As we said earlier, boundaries, processes, standards, and ethics are important to the successful management of any organization. To be effective, they need to be clearly stated in terms of their purposes and their implementation. They need to engage the power of boundaries.

Boundaries and standards clearly delineated enable hidden leaders to make the most of their creative problem-solving skills. By knowing the purpose of existing processes and standards, hidden leaders are better equipped to make intelligent decisions about how to alter standards to meet the goal for the customer.

Just as artists, given tight project boundaries, employ new levels of creativity their artwork, hidden leaders working within clearly defined structures find creative ways to reach their goals. They can stretch existing structural limitations without threatening the integrity of the system as a whole.

In any competitive environment, innovation is often touted as the solution to tough issues concerning products, services, and progress. In many cases, employers ask workers to innovate while still doing more with less in terms of time, resources, and staff. In these situations, where the boundaries are especially strict, hidden leaders rise to the occasion, using their independent initiative to break the box that seems to limit their solutions at first glance.

For example, in 2007, long before social media were seen as anything but college students' playthings, the external-affairs team of a Fortune 500 telecommunications company discovered the power of social media to support the company's position in a local election. The team wanted to raise awareness about the negative implications of a proposed telephone tax. While the team's managers recognized the issue as of some importance, they gave the team no budget for the project at the city level because of regional and national funding priorities. The team also didn't have much time: It was facing a city council vote in forty-five days.

Team members knew they had to present the issues to the public. However, the commonly accepted box of corporate communications was closed to them. And time was of the essence.

The team's hidden leaders stepped up. First, they redefined their goal as one of communicating critical information to a wide public audience in a short amount of time. They connected the effects of their recent personal uses of Twitter and Facebook to the team's goal of reaching its audience. Within a few days, they were reinventing social media as a tool for public relations.

The team created a Facebook page for the campaign and used email distribution lists to drive traffic to it. It established a Twitter account and actively recruited followers with messages about rejecting the phone tax. Keeping the informative content fresh took only minutes each day and easily scaled their efforts. Both Twitter and Facebook were relatively new, so the approach of using this new medium for business purposes garnered attention. The team's limits—no money and little time—forced its creativity. The limits also helped the team transcend the usual corporate approaches to public relations.

Did the team win that first city council vote? In fact, no. But the prototype use of social media became the company's model for many future campaigns that did influence city and county governments' policies toward the company.

A few years later, social media were more integrated into most companies' public relations and policy programs. The independent initiative of this team of hidden leaders helped spark that trend because they chose to destroy the box of traditional corporate communication tools.

Where boundaries drive creativity, context enables hidden leaders to promote the organization's goals and strategies while fulfilling job requirements. By context, we mean ensuring that employees are clear on management's big picture strategic goals and understand the links between employees' tactical actions and management's strategic aims.

Without context—and we see many organizations that suffer from this—employees may be at cross-purposes. They may not understand how their tactical actions affect the long-term goals of the company and the value promise to the organization's paying customers. Providing context is a management communications responsibility. As with initiatives and strategies, this context is not a one-time communication but ongoing connection of strategic vision to tactical actions throughout the organization.

When hidden leaders are clear on the context of their job responsibilities, they are able to make decisions and invent ideas that support the long-term goals of the company. They align their contributions to those of management. When context is clear, each employee can do this. Because hidden leaders focus on results, they especially benefit from a clear contextual understanding. Because hidden leaders may be altering the means to reach goals, by understanding the context of the company's overall strategy they can ensure that those means do not contradict major strategic ideas.

Without context, employees are limited in their abilities to contribute to a company's success. With context, hidden leaders especially see connections between opportunities and make their work results more meaningful to themselves and to the organization.

Early in his career, Scott worked for the professional services firm Coopers & Lybrand (which ultimately became PricewaterhouseCoopers). The partner he was assigned to, Chris Abramson, was in charge of human resource management for the San Francisco and Bay Area offices. Chris had an enormous amount of responsibility in spite of being in a position most often seen as merely administrative.

As an associate in the firm, Scott had limited interactions with partners. He noticed, however, that whenever he was face-to-face with Chris, the partner would give him his undivided attention. Chris talked with Scott about his career and opportunities for growth. He traded stories about events and people outside the office. In short conversations, when Chris was directing Scott to do something, Chris injected some kind of personal remark or comment.

Chris's ability to engage with other partners and managers in the firm enabled him to help the people who worked for him, including Scott, when challenges arose. His knack for connecting with other partners as individuals—not as generators of billable hours or problem-solving resources, but as people—was the key to resolving the majority of conflicts that arose. Because of his authentic interest in others and his ability to lead through relationships, Chris succeeded as an effective leader with a major impact on the firm's success.

Remains Customer Purposed

Being customer purposed is different from providing customer service or being customer driven. It entails an awareness of how an action in a specific job affects the customer. By customer, we specifically mean the customer who pays the bills.

Being customer purposed means seeing the big picture of the company's value promise and acting in ways that enable that promise. This is more than a sense of "customer service," which implies that the one serving the customer will do anything to make the customer happy (possibly to the company's detriment). Customer-purposed hidden leaders who rarely meet their company's paying customers consistently think about how their own actions, products, and services affect those customers. They interpret their work in terms of how they might improve life for the customer who pays.

The primary distinction of customer-purposed hidden leaders is that they focus on delivering their company's value promise during every aspect of the customer experience. This is more than being solely concerned with transactions or the hidden leader's role in them. Plenty of options exist to be "good enough" or even (that dreadful phrase) to "exceed expectations" during transactions involving products and services. Customer-purposed hidden leaders recognize the importance of the entire customer experience and how actions by everyone in the organization affect it.

A sense of being customer purposed extends everyone's responsibilities to ensure that the customer receives value. For example, Scott lives in Florida, and, like many others in that state, he has a pool. He hired a company to maintain the pool: to clean it, balance various chemicals to keep it sanitary, and make sure various pumps were working properly.

All went well for a time. Then Scott experienced some problems. Chlorine levels were too high. The pumps were not cycling on and off properly. After a few weeks of this, Scott decided it was time to talk with someone at the service company.

Initially, he approached various staff members who worked on the pool. Over a month, he discovered that the pool company routinely assigned different people to work on his pool. Depending on the week, Scott heard different answers. One maintenance person said it was the filtration system. A week later, another claimed the chemical mix was wrong. The third week, a worker said everything looked fine. So Scott got no consistent answers.

Scott then called the pool crew's supervisor. The supervisor came over and ran some tests on Scott's pool, including checking the pump system. He told Scott he could find nothing wrong. After the supervisor left, Scott called the territory manager, who suggested there might be a water-circulation problem related to the pool's pump. If that were the problem, Scott would have to deal directly with the manufacturer; since the pool-maintenance company didn't install the pump, it could not take responsibility for it.

Frustrated, Scott lamented the fact that no one on the maintenance crew or in the company seemed to care enough to provide a clear view of the problem and a solution—though the company claimed to be a specialist in pool maintenance. Ultimately, Scott switched pool-maintenance companies. He found a team that seemed to actually care about servicing the pool effectively and solving pool-performance issues for him before they became a nuisance.

The crew from the first company probably was well trained in pool maintenance. The supervisor knew how to motivate its members and get them working. Most likely, the company focused on the technical aspects of crew members' work. But no one in the company seemed to be aware of the real value of the company to the customer. No one saw his job as including making the customer happy. That task always belonged to someone else. Furthermore, none of them saw it as their job to find out who "someone else" was. They were not customer purposed.

For example, a major financial services company was struggling to broaden its market share. As part of its efforts, the CEO directed a complete culture change to make the organization more customer focused. We've seen plenty of organizations give lip service to similar initiatives, largely serving up platitudes about customer centricity and client focus. However, in this successful transformation, everyone in the organization worked on pragmatic approaches that oriented them to customers' experiences. They clearly knew how their work affected customers, regardless of whether or not it directly involved them.

One administrative assistant who participated in our work was quick to acknowledge that she was often the first person many people encountered in the organization. Being customer purposed, she knew that these interactions set the tone for how people would experience the company. Clear on the customer-focus initiative, she maintained an optimistic and positive demeanor with all colleagues, stakeholders, and customers.

While many people in a similar position might see themselves simply as administrators, this hidden leader understood that fulfilling her role helped the whole organization run smoothly for its customers and stakeholders. Without her, meetings might be jumbled on calendars, managers might not know where or when important events were being held, and documents might be sloppy and lack attention to detail.

"As a customer-focused company, that is not the kind of image we want to project," she told us in an interview, "and I am responsible for that. A big part of my job is helping create a new culture for this company." As a customer-purposed hidden leader, she translated how her daily friendliness, attention to detail, and skilled follow-up created the new culture for this growing financial institution, a new culture that was essential to its future success.

CHAPTER TWO

Identify Hidden Leaders

We have identified four facets of hidden leadership, with specific, observable behaviors that might indicate a hidden leader at work. The perfect and fully developed hidden leader displays all these behaviors. However, no one is a perfect specimen of any given characteristic. Everyone can be placed on a continuum of behaviors. How do you, as a manager, look at a person as a whole and identify potential as a hidden leader?

WHEN ONE CHARACTERISTIC IS MISSING

While, ideally, potential hidden leaders you have identified will exhibit integrity and some element of the remaining three aspects, you may notice people you think are leaders who are strong in only two aspects, or perhaps one. Without developing the missing characteristics, it is unlikely that hidden leaders will fulfill their potential. It's similar to sitting on a three-legged stool with one short leg. No matter how good your balance, your stool will be weak in one direction. The same is true of hidden leaders.

This is not to say that, given demonstrated integrity and at least two characteristics, a hidden leader cannot be developed. But how can a manager know if a particular person has the potential for hidden leadership in spite of skill deficits?

When two of the three characteristics are present, you will see distinctive roles and reputations in potential hidden leaders. We have identified them as the short-term visionary, the busywork-er, and the lone wolf (see Figure 2-1). Each of these types lacks one of the key characteristics of the true hidden leader.

*Figure 2-1: Venn diagram of the varieties of hidden leadership,
based on the three key characteristics.*

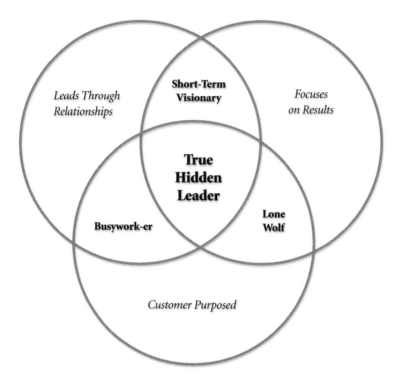

By evaluating each potential hidden leader's integrity and knowing how each person might respond to development and investment, a manager can identify the less-than-perfect hidden leaders in the organization who still can be coached to provide important leadership in the company.

Let's see how you can identify potential hidden leaders who are missing one of the three key characteristics of the true hidden leader.

The *short-term visionary* combines results and relationships to produce action. Generally, these workers are effective in getting things done—at least things relevant to the short-term success of the company. They are continually in achievement mode, clicking off tasks, completing assignments, and accomplishing goals, all while keeping relationships intact.

However, the short-term visionary is missing the customer-purposed characteristics of a true hidden leader. This frequently leads to actions that produce short-term gains at the expense of long-term results.

Because they are not customer purposed, these potential hidden leaders lack the voice of the customer in their actions. As a result, they are in danger of making decisions that address localized, internal issues at the expense of customers.

For instance, a desk clerk at a hotel may choose not to make a concession for a frequent guest, with the idea of saving the company money. Doing so improves the organization's profitability, at least for that night. Because the clerk authentically built a comfortable relationship with the night's customer and put no internal relationships at risk, she may be seen as a good team player because she makes decisions based on the internal goals of the business. But by not recognizing an opportunity to act with the customer in mind, she may have also sacrificed an opportunity to build that customer's long-term loyalty and, with it, the organization's profitability beyond one night.

Some of these customer-purposed decisions are enabled or hampered by the policies of the company itself. For example, some hotel chains do not give their clerks (or managers) any flexibility with rates or special requests. In those cases, to expect that a hidden leader would act with the customer in mind—and still have a job after a few instances of breaking the rules—is wishful thinking on the part of the organization's management. If you as a manager see many short-term visionaries around you, all trying to do a great job, you may consider looking at the policies and procedures that inhibit these people's abilities to blossom into full-fledged hidden leaders by being customer purposed.

The hospitality world includes one company that is cognizant of every employee's ability to be customer purposed in the right situation. The Ritz-Carlton hotel chain is famous for its customer-purposed culture. Every person, including those on the housekeeping staff, receives intensive training, development, and encouragement from all levels of management to provide the customer service for which the company is famous.

One policy in place throughout the hotel chain is that each employee, including housekeeping staff (we refer to housekeeping again because, for some reason, many people do not consider them important to the customer's experience of a hotel), is authorized to spend up to $50 a night of the hotel's money on any overnight guest to create an experience that makes for a happy customer. It may entail replacing a ruined shirt, or buying shoes to stand in for ones forgotten at home. The policy is whatever it takes—and the freedom to spend $50, no questions asked. That is a policy that enables hidden leaders to act on their customer-purposed instincts.

Without customer purpose present, eventually, the short-term visionary, effective as he may be in the moment, misses the big picture. In doing so, he cannot act out the value promise of the organization.

We don't imply that short-term results aren't critical to any organization. As we aim for the long term, it is short-term success that gets us there. No company can reach its long-term markers of success without passing the short-term markers along the way. But failing to meet customer objectives at the same time makes ever reaching our long-term objectives nearly impossible.

When you as a manager see short-term visionaries, remember that a customer-purposed attitude can be developed. Do not discount the importance of people with strong relationships throughout the organization and an ability to focus on results.

Have you ever noticed an employee who is incredibly busy but seems to contribute very little to the company's long-term success? These well-intended professionals frequently have good relationships and exhibit a strong customer purpose. They certainly display a good work ethic, and they do get things done, especially routine assignments or marginally important projects. But without a focus on results, odds are that these workers will accomplish very little that contributes much to the value desired by customers or the long-term health of the organization. We call these potential leaders *busywork-ers.*

The busywork-er lacks the characteristic of a focus on results. Without that focus, the person has no yardstick by which to measure the importance of specific tasks. Many busywork-ers have tremendous planning and execution skills, as well as excellent relationships. They do maintain the centrality of the customer, which helps them make tactical decisions. But without the end game in mind, they may expend energy on projects and ideas that are good but not as valuable as they might be to the organization or the customer. They get results, but the results may not be in line with the company's strategic objectives.

Without a focus on results, the busywork-er risks having all of her work devolve to a task without aim. In other words, work for work's sake. Sometimes, of course, certain work must be done, and done well and on time, that is important to the organization as a whole. But the busywork-er in that position who cannot evaluate based on a focus on results will not become a hidden leader.

For example, a human resources staff person may be a firm believer in the organization's promise to customers and possess strong relationships across the organization. He has two of the important characteristics of a hidden leader. But without a focus on results, he often gets mired in tasks and overwhelmed by priorities. He has trouble determining which of many responsibilities actually contribute in a meaningful way to long-term business results. His ideas and suggestions often miss the mark in terms of driving the organization toward its strategic goals. Everyone likes him because of his strong relationships, but he is not often called on to brainstorm solutions to thorny issues that are critical to the company's success.

Some of this evidence of a busywork-er—confused priorities or a lack of significant contribution—can also be created when an organization fails to either communicate the results desired or changes the end game frequently. If you see many busywork-ers among your staff or in your company, look critically at how upper management is communicating the results desired for the company. Does the C-level consistently change the strategic vision? Is the vision too vague to be translated into tactical goals? Do executives ignore the importance of communicating a strong vision to all levels of the organization? Is that communication tardy, unclear, a one-off event, or contrary to previous vision statements? If the answer to any of these questions is "yes," your lack of hidden leaders and glut of busywork-ers may be a structural problem in your organization.

For example, before news sources commonly accepted the importance of an online presence, we worked with a large New England newspaper struggling to compete in a changing market. Key competitors had already taken a chunk out of the paper's ad revenue through their websites. Some were local newspapers, but others were former or specialized ad sheets that catered to niche audiences.

The newspaper's CEO assigned an online group to create a website that would recapture this ad revenue. But the CEO insisted that the site couldn't take ads away from the printed product, nor could it upstage the paper with original stories. The CEO did not communicate or discuss a clear vision of what the website should be. Clearly, management saw the website as a second-tier stepchild of the newspaper.

Undaunted by this status, the team was enthusiastic. Said one team member, "We felt we were defining something new for the industry. But the goal set for us by management seemed contradictory: nothing new or free, but create ad revenue.

"We went around in circles. We had vision meetings, created slide decks of business models, and the programmers—we asked them for scores of sample pages, trying to find our product. We worked almost around the clock to meet internal deadlines. It wasn't uncommon for meetings to be interrupted, or for programmers to take on competing priorities.

"In the end, we produced online access to the newspaper for existing subscribers, complete with firewall and passwords. But from the start, ad-vertisers didn't want to pay for online ads that already were in the newspa-per, and subscribers tended to want the physical product, since the experi-ence of the two was essentially the same. When traffic to the site dissolved, we were frustrated. All that work, and nothing, really, to show for it."

Clearly, the CEO and other managers, struggling with falling revenues, did not see the website as a player in the process of regaining market share. They did not help develop or communicate a vision for what the website might be. In essence, without this support for its work, the team wasted time trying to discover a vision through trial and error. Team members had talent, skills, and enthusiasm. They lacked clear priorities and a vision supported by the overall goals of the newspaper. The result was a lot of busywork for people who could have contributed much more to the paper's success.

The ability of a busywork-er to connect his work to specific company strategies, goals, and objectives would make a huge difference in his contributions to the company. It would also make that person an effective hidden leader. Fortunately, a focus on results can be learned. It does require structural support within the organization, but given that, managers can develop busywork-ers into hidden leaders with development and training.

We've seen that a focus on results is important to evaluate what work to get done. Being customer purposed provides another measure to ascertain what's important for the success of the customer and the company. Absent the ability or interest to develop productive and positive relationships, however, a worker limits his success. We call a potential hidden leader who lacks the ability to lead through relationships a *lone wolf*.

In some situations, a lone wolf can be an asset. Especially where technical requirements are key, a lone wolf can accept an assignment, understand its importance, and do it well. Many people with specialized or concentrated knowledge in a variety of fields, from software development to finance to law to medicine, fall into this category and produce great work for a company. It may be the cornerstone of a product's success. But lone wolves are unlikely to develop into hidden leaders.

Without support from others in an organization, it is difficult for anyone to provide effective leadership. Project work generally occurs horizontally in companies. That is, many projects involve different functions, often organized vertically, that rarely interact with one another. (Thus the term *silos* to describe such functions in an organization.) To lead effectively, a hidden leader must garner support across these silos and work with multiple constituencies among different functions in the organization. Lacking that ability, the hidden leader is reduced to a lone wolf: an effective and productive person but not someone considered to be a leader.

For example, a product-development associate in a manufacturing company may be gifted in her ability to understand and engineer solutions to customer problems. She may be very organized because she is so results oriented. But if she can't cultivate positive relationships with others in her department or throughout the organization, she will be unlikely to collaborate with others. She may be capable, and pose good ideas, but lacking good relationships will limit her effectiveness. She is likely to miss out on insights and input from colleagues that could improve her work, or lose opportunities to see her hard work adopted by the organization.

The most common lone wolf behavior we've seen is that of the rogue sales professional. Generally, this person is very results focused and customer purposed and may achieve good sales results. But the customer is his primary target: He puts little effort or energy into developing relationships with colleagues.

Others in the organization complain that this person often doesn't cooperate with marketing and has conflicts with people in accounting or product delivery. He tends to have more difficulty resolving organizational issues for customers in such areas as on-time delivery, product quality, or billing. He can also create problems in the organization that may increase costs. Compare these behaviors with those of salespeople who have effective relationships with other departments. Issues affecting their customers are resolved smoothly and with less organizational strain.

The irony here is that successful lone wolf salespeople have reasonable relationship-development skills; they simply do not aim them at their co-workers.

Absent connections through relationships, the lone wolf also makes work more difficult because he has trouble getting others to support even his best ideas. He may tend to work behind the scenes to get around committees, leaders, and task forces. This may build a reputation of being an outlier, especially if the lone wolf's work is essentially strong. Then this person becomes someone to manage closely, not someone to see as a potential leader within the organization.

If you see lone wolves predominating in your organization, you may be seeing evidence of a cultural communications problem. How often do relationships devolve into backbiting or political struggles? How well are people acknowledged and commended publicly for their work? Who gets the credit when credit is due? How honest and forthright are C-level executives perceived to be? Answering these questions can help you determine if the only way to survive in your company's culture is to be a lone wolf. In that case, managers will have trouble finding and developing hidden leaders because the culture does not value the importance of developing relationships.

For example, Scott was working with a venture-backed biotech start-up. Rapidly growing with new innovations, the company had increased its employee base tenfold in just two years. Executive management stated a key value as "mutual respect for each other." A widely understood responsibility based on this value was that if someone experienced a problem with another person, it was the first person's responsibility to try to work it out before taking the conflict to the next level of management.

This rule of responsibility was endemic in the culture. If someone discussed a personal conflict with a third person, the standard first response was, "Have you talked with the person about this?" If the answer was no, then without any gossip, the protocol was to simply suggest that action. The combination of practicing those two elements (not just giving lip service to them) created an environment that placed high value on developing constructive relationships, a massive enhancer of productivity.

At one point, the company ran into difficulty getting a new product to market. As critical deadlines passed, tensions ran high and some finger pointing began. After a particular series of problems, two frontline lab technicians volunteered to document the failure points in the project. Because these two techs had developed good relationships with colleagues in clinical marketing and R&D, they could gather information that otherwise would have been difficult to obtain. Recognizing this, people in other departments were willing to collaborate with them. The tone and tenor of these relationships enabled the techs—obviously two hidden leaders—to sort out disagreements and inconsistencies by seeking cause, not blame. Not only were the lab techs able to identify technical problems, communication breakdowns, and process glitches, they discovered new information that enabled them to recommend multiple ways to tackle the issues. Management adopted nearly every one of those suggestions.

Eight months later, the release of the new diagnostic product was tremendously successful. The company increased its revenue by more than 40 percent in the next two quarters. As a result of her efforts, one of the lab techs was offered a promotion to lab manager, which she accepted. The other, for personal reasons, declined a similar opportunity the following year. A few of her colleagues jokingly—but respectfully—refer to her as "first among equals."

In most organizations, it takes more than one person to achieve an objective. In classical sales organizations, where individuals close sales without significant staff support, the collaboration of others helps sales professionals market, deliver, collect, and service accounts. No one can drive organizational success alone.

Sometimes technical brilliance is able to stand on its own. More often, though, it is a result of people working productively together to produce results. Without leading through relationships, a hidden leader cannot emerge.

WHEN ONE CHARACTERISTIC DOMINATES

In our experience, hidden leaders rarely display only one of the three characteristics of leading through relationships, focusing on results, and being customer purposed. However, there are times when one element predominates in how a person works in the organization.

When leading through relationships is all-important to a person, we see the "nice guy" emerge, the employee who may not have technical skills or a focus on results or the customer but whom everyone likes. Unfortunately, often these nice guys are shuffled around organizations because no one has the heart to demand better performance or let them go. We have worked with managers who agonize for months or years over what to do with these professionals because they like them as people but struggle with the amount of value they create for the organization.

One executive at a Fortune 500 computer hardware manufacturer told us that a particular nice guy in his organization was hard to release because he was so well connected and liked. The executive was concerned about the damage to his own reputation for terminating such a popular employee. Staff may like the nice guy in a management role, but often they must go around him to actually get things done.

A zealous focus on results creates a person we call a driver. While on the surface it seems an organization would love drivers, they can be very disruptive. In the short run, the driver may earn the respect of others, but such an employee will not be able to be a hidden leader.

On one coaching assignment, we were called in to work with a manager who was very successful at achieving most of the objectives put before her. She hit her numbers and attained budget targets. Unfortunately, as her manager put it, she wrought so much havoc among others in reaching those goals that many questioned whether she was worth the hassle.

Organizations value customer focus, but when being customer purposed is the primary characteristic of a worker, she is seen as a warrior. These individuals are often zealous advocates for clients and will do anything to satisfy a customer need or request—although some actions may be at the expense of doing what is right for the organization. In the worst cases, customer needs are used to push a specific agenda unrelated to what the customer truly wants.

We worked with one consumer packaged-goods company whose marketing group suffered greatly from this warrior syndrome. Many of marketing's supervisors and managers were notorious for criticizing everything the organization did to help customers (except marketing of course). This attitude created rifts between marketing and other divisions. It drove a wedge between areas in the company that should have been allies in providing value to customers.

As a manager, should you try to convert the nice guys, drivers, and warriors into hidden leaders? Perhaps. Depending on your leadership needs and situation, some of these potential leaders may be worth the investment of training and coaching required to develop them into hidden leaders, especially if they are already in management ranks. For example, if a driver who is a manager has immense business savvy and vision critical to the company and is open to personal and professional growth, the investment to develop the person's relational and customer-purpose skills may be worth it.

On the other hand, it is our experience that many more people lack only minimal critical characteristics to be hidden leaders. Some may lack one characteristic completely; others may have all three but may need development of two to a higher level of expertise. These are the potential hidden leaders from whose development you are more likely to get the most substantial return on investment.

The first facet of hidden leadership we discussed in this book was demonstrating integrity. It's the context within which all hidden leaders—and many obvious leaders—operate.

In our view, there is no potential for a hidden leader who does not demonstrate integrity. This characteristic is observable, but trying to teach an adult integrity is attempting to counteract years of early training and self-awareness. We, like most managers, are not professional psychiatrists. Yet in our experience, it is not possible to train a person without integrity to develop and then regularly demonstrate integrity. Those who embrace a "certain moral flexibility" are not candidates for hidden leadership. Those who believe they can "get away with it" will continue to do so in spite of any training short of legal incarceration. We hope you as a manager don't have to deal with that level of unethical behavior! It's not the manager's job to teach people how to improve their moral judgment. But it is the manager's responsibility to help those with integrity develop the courage to demonstrate it. Employees who feel shy or intimidated or express concern privately can be coached to speak up in more public venues, like meetings. When they do, it's the manager's role to commend and support their efforts to demonstrate what they clearly embrace.

Many organizations claim integrity as a value. At issue is how they personify it. If integrity is endemic to the culture, it manifests itself in hidden leaders who demonstrate it consistently. It also emerges from positional leaders—managers, executives, and others—who have the courage to say, "This action is not in the best interests of our customer."

On the other hand, there are organizations that say they embrace integrity but essentially mistrust their managers and supervisors to select people who fit into the organization's culture. Many of these companies use so-called personality or psychometric tests as part of their hiring processes or as ways to build better communication skills among existing employees.

There are hosts of these tests, including Myers-Briggs, DiSC, and other "research-based" social-style tests and tools. Typically we see them used to label people and explain away bad behavior or poor skills. We've heard statements in these companies like, "Oh, he's an ENTJ; what do you expect?"

We think this is simply lazy management. Further, we doubt the efficacy of the tests in telling anyone anything about their personalities. Seeing their results, test takers say, "Oh this is so like me!" Of course it is: They filled out the questionnaire. It doesn't mean they will always respond that way, or that their personality is fixed in time and space.

Test results seem true because individuals look at them through the lens of their inner selves. They resemble astrology columns, which always apply to everyone's vision of his day, no matter the sign. (Some such columns are invented by random people assigned to write them, like Laurie's husband in his college days.)

Anne Murphy Paul, in her book *The Cult of Personality Testing*, agrees. She writes, "As many as three-quarters of test takers achieve a different personality type when tested again, and . . . the sixteen distinctive personality types described by the Myers-Briggs have no scientific basis whatsoever."[1] Using personality tests is a way to avoid the responsibility of selecting, hiring, or coaching employees so they can succeed in their jobs. It's also a sign that integrity, however promoted, may be lacking in the culture as a whole.

WORKSHEET: EVALUATE A HIDDEN LEADER

bit.ly/16Mu2hD

The better you can pinpoint a hidden leader's strengths, the easier it will be to develop missing skills and characteristics. Think of a specific person, and then review the pages that follow. Check the behaviors you have observed in all four areas: has integrity that shows, leads through relationships, focuses on results, and is customer purposed. The more checkmarks in each level, the more developed your hidden leader's abilities. The online worksheet will calculate this for you.

Notice that when you evaluate integrity that shows, you are evaluating both the hidden leader's ability to show integrity and others' perception of that integrity. There are no levels of integrity per se, because there are no variations on integrity. One has integrity or not. In terms of evaluating the hidden leader, then, you are simply evaluating that leader's ability to show the integrity that already exists within the leader's personality.

EVALUATE A HIDDEN LEADER: HAS INTEGRITY THAT SHOWS
Description: Has the courage to consistently adhere to a strong ethical code, even in difficult situations.

Behaviors of the hidden leader

Observed Behaviors	Evaluate: Yes or No
Carefully evaluates before making promises that will be hard to fulfill	
Keeps commitments regularly	
Matches actions to verbal commitments	
Informs colleagues regularly about changing workloads or deadlines	
Consistently adheres to a strong personal ethical code	
Acts in accordance with company values	
Addresses potential ethical issues before they become major problems	
Makes ethical decisions consistently	
Speaks up when integrity issues are on the table, even if they are unpopular	
Describes both sides of an issue or argument	
Confronts others who act unethically or dishonestly	

Behaviors of the hidden leader's colleagues

Observed Behaviors	Evaluate: Yes or No
Trusts the hidden leader to act in the best interests of the organization, its employees, and its customers	
Describes hidden leader's treatment of others as fair and honest	
Models personal ethical behavior on that of the hidden leader	
Identifies the hidden leader as a good resource to help resolve disputes, clarify ambiguous situations, and address challenges	
Describes support from the hidden leader for efforts, accomplishments, and professional development	

(Continued)

EVALUATE A HIDDEN LEADER: LEADS THROUGH RELATIONSHIPS
Description:

- Uses interpersonal skills effectively
- Exercises a sense of curiosity
- Values others
- Believes in personal value to others, whether as a co-worker or as a friend

Observed Behaviors

Level 1	Level 2	Level 3	Level 4
❑ Appears approachable and friendly ❑ Seeks the opinions of colleagues ❑ Actively develops new relationships across the organization ❑ Credits others privately for successes and contributions ❑ Communicates to supervisor appropriately concerning colleagues and work issues	❑ Establishes strong rapport with colleagues ❑ Works comfortably with colleagues to complete assignments ❑ Handles challenging situations without raising negative emotions in self, reducing conflict ❑ Demonstrates respect for others in public ❑ Gives honest and balanced feedback appropriately when asked ❑ Communicates to management appropriately concerning colleagues and work issues	❑ Asks questions to understand colleagues' issues and concerns ❑ Helps to manage conflict in his or her work group without raising negative emotions in others ❑ Helps others understand his or her thought process, making connections for listeners between important points ❑ Credits others publicly for successes and contributions ❑ Involves colleagues who appear shy or hesitant in discussions and conversations	❑ Promotes collaboration and teamwork throughout the company ❑ Manages conflict effectively at many levels throughout the company ❑ Connects with people in other teams or divisions that help improve results for the business ❑ Offers honest and balanced feedback appropriately ❑ Shares relevant information broadly throughout the organization

(Continued)

EVALUATE A HIDDEN LEADER: A FOCUS ON RESULTS
Description: Uses the ends to define the means to achieve a goal, and maintains independent initiative to act.

Observed Behaviors

Level 1	Level 2	Level 3	Level 4
❑ Maintains initiative to achieve assigned objectives ❑ Focuses actions on business priorities and goals ❑ Effectively addresses barriers to goals ❑ Expresses personal commitment to achieve assigned objectives	❑ Displays a sense of urgency for achieving goals ❑ Meets commitments to attain goals ❑ Suggests new ways to improve efficiency and productivity ❑ Ensures that goals describe outcomes rather than process or input ❑ Productive beyond routine assignments	❑ Asks questions to determine the best processes to achieve results ❑ Adjusts or stretches process steps to achieve goals ❑ Describes end goals in terms of results ❑ Identifies a variety of actions that will achieve a goal ❑ Sets effective priorities to meet business goals and customer needs	❑ Provides ideas and information that influence the goals of the business ❑ Suggests procedural improvements to achieve results for customers ❑ Describes critical measures that most affect the company's performance

(Continued)

EVALUATE A HIDDEN LEADER: IS CUSTOMER PURPOSED

Description: Sees the big picture of the company's value promise and acts in ways that enable that promise for the paying customer.

Observed Behaviors

Level 1	Level 2	Level 3	Level 4
❏ Shows authentic enthusiasm for the job	❏ Demonstrates passion for delivering value to the customer who pays	❏ Encourages others to link their work to the value promise of the organization	❏ Promotes loyalty to the organization based on its value promise and values
❏ Demonstrates adequate communication and technical job skills	❏ Demonstrates an equal balance of average communication and technical job skills	❏ Demonstrates a balance of above-average communication and technical skills	❏ Demonstrates an equal balance of exceptional communication and technical skills
❏ Asks for help when skills are inadequate or situations are challenging	❏ Asks for help when skills are inadequate or situations are challenging	❏ Cultivates customer relationships that provide insight into potential improvements	❏ Suggests ways to adapt company strategy to support customer expectations
❏ Describes how customers experience the organization	❏ Routinely interacts with customers to get feedback on business performance	❏ Uses customer data to influence business objectives	❏ Looks for ways to keep up with changes in the marketplace or customer base
❏ Describes the importance of making a difference for customers	❏ Displays a sense of urgency for achieving goals	❏ Prompts a sense of urgency in others to meet customer needs	❏ Promotes change initiatives by helping others commit to the change
❏ Responds rapidly to customer needs and concerns	❏ Helps others understand the need for major changes in process or market approach	❏ Supports change initiatives by integrating initiative goals into actions	
❏ Accepts change initiatives in performing job responsibilities			

CHAPTER THREE

Enable Integrity

Each of us likes to believe we have integrity. Many of us do. But how does an organization ensure that its corporate culture recognizes, supports, and enables high integrity? When hidden leaders demonstrate integrity, they provide an opportunity for everyone to demonstrate and support integrity, too. By knowing integrity when you see it demonstrated by these leaders, you can determine the best ways to personally support it. You can also determine how well your company culture supports it and use specific tactics to enable integrity throughout the culture.

HOW DO YOU RECOGNIZE INTEGRITY?

When a hidden leader demonstrates integrity, she courageously and consistently adheres to a strong ethical code. Whenever one meets a hidden leader, the integrity is obvious in the leader's conversations, suggestions, responses, and actions. While hidden leaders display integrity in all their activities, sometimes much of their work is done in solitude or within a small group. This can make it difficult for those uninvolved in the team to see the leader's integrity in action.

The challenge for managers is observing visible evidence of integrity when the hidden leader is not in the immediate vicinity. In many cases, the manager must watch and listen for this evidence in the comments, responses, and actions of others—those who depend on hidden leaders in the organization and know the leaders' integrity can be depended on in the toughest situations.

For example, Scott was helping a boutique training firm develop and implement a cohesive strategy, part of which was a new training program created by the firm's owners. They were very proud of it and planned to make it their keystone product.

A number of the employees in the firm had privately confided in Scott that they felt the program, as designed, could not deliver on its promise. In their opinions, it did not address the learning objectives and performance outcome it promised. These employees were concerned that clients would not be happy with the result.

At a meeting to discuss the program's launch, most employees of the firm, including the ones who had confided in Scott, feigned praise or said nothing. They were concerned that the owners would not take their criticisms well.

One client representative, Susan, was the only person to take a hidden-leader approach. Courageously, she pointed out that from her perspective as a client representative, the program was not in the best interests of the company's clients because it would not produce the improved business results the firm touted.

Just as the rest of the employees suspected, the owners of the firm did not respond well. They began to argue hotly with Susan that she didn't know what she was talking about and they had done a lot of research and careful development to make the program work. In spite of these arguments, Susan maintained her position, citing examples of client issues that supported her argument.

Susan's courage and integrity in making an unpopular argument for the sake of the customer galvanized others in the room. Other employees rose to defend Susan's points and share their own criticisms. The owners became quiet and ultimately listened. Faced with the overwhelming anecdotal evidence that the program needed more work, the owners agreed to revamp the program before launching it.

Susan's ability to stand up for what she felt was right—making an unpopular argument for the sake of the customer—led to a better product and ultimately more satisfied clients. Being a hidden leader was not easy for her, but in the end she gained the respect of her peers and senior management and ensured that customers got a better result. She also changed the beliefs of many in the company about acceptable ways to disagree with the company's founders and still collaborate to create a productive end result.

While the owners of this company were slow to heed Susan's leadership, the support garnered from others finally enabled them to see its value. The redesigned program, once launched, was successfully adopted by many of the organization's current clients and a significant number of new ones. Careful observation and listening in situations like these can point to hidden leaders in an organization. Following are a few examples of situations where we believe hidden leaders can be discovered through the comments, actions, and recommendations of others.

Because hidden leaders demonstrate integrity, others trust that those leaders will meet their commitments. In the business world, this makes hidden leaders a dependable resource when deadlines are tight or situations are difficult. Because hidden leaders also have the courage to act, they can be counted on to help solve problems. Some of those problems may be outside of the leaders' immediate areas of responsibility.

When a manager hears employees suggest solutions that consistently include asking for help from a specific individual, that individual may be a hidden leader known to everyone on the front line. For example, suppose a team is overloaded and needs to offload a specific task or decision, or find a way to get more resources for the job. When those teams consistently point to one person not on the team who can help address the issue, investigate that person as a potential hidden leader.

Because of the leader's integrity, team members know they can depend on this person to get a task done, ask management for resources, or tell the team the truth about other options for handling those tasks. For example, Laurie was facilitating a strategy session with a number of frontline supervisors and lower-level managers who were asked to develop a competency-training plan for a new sales force. One of the managers proposed that a large group of skills was necessary before a salesperson could even begin to speak with customers. The group hesitated but generally concurred.

Another manager pointed out that training newly hired salespeople to succeed would be expensive and time consuming. In light of recent market challenges, it would negate the company's products' competitive advantages. After a short silence, one of the supervisors took an alternate stand. She proposed that with only a few of those skills, a newly hired salesperson could at least go out on sales calls and shadow an experienced salesperson to learn more about how to interact with customers. In that way, the new person could potentially contribute to the sale and would learn critical skills quickly. Further, if new salespeople were then offered a group of simpler products to sell, with shorter sales cycles, they could practice critical skills in less competitive arenas. At the same time, they could continue their training to build more complex skills.

The hidden leader in this situation—the supervisor with the alternate plan—listened to everyone's points of view, proposed a solution that did not negate the need for highly trained salespeople, and enabled the company to bring new hires along faster. She presented her ideas freely, although the final proposal in front of the group came from someone higher in her organization. Her courage to speak up enabled the group to address a challenge effectively.

Many decisions in organizations do not entail clear or obvious choices. That's why such decisions are important and difficult. Someone must judge or weigh the alternatives to identify the best result for the largest number of people and the goals of the organization.

Most decisions offer a range of possibilities, including options that blur distinctions between right and wrong or best and worst. These ambiguous situations make many people uncomfortable. Evaluating a situation and identifying the critical elements before beginning the decision-making process requires a clear sense of one's own ethical code. It also requires an ability to acknowledge and accept the unknowns related to the decision. These unknowns create ambiguity, a lack of certainty that, to some, makes these decisions tantamount to flipping a coin.

In our experience, hidden leaders manage this ambiguity well, both personally and professionally. For example, pressed by deadlines but without full knowledge of a customer's needs, a team was struggling with how to proceed. One faction wanted to stop the project until all information could be obtained; another felt that some kind of progress had to be made now. A hidden leader on the team suggested identifying what was already determined and presenting that by the deadline while approaching the customer for more information to be included in a later version.

Hidden leaders may not make the right decisions every time, but they are able to make decisions, a trait that in high-level executives is a signal of future success. Doing something—anything—achieves results faster than trying to eliminate ambiguity with facts, research, or knowledge. As Rosabeth Moss Kanter points out, perfection is unattainable anyway.[1] Hidden leaders know this. They depend on their integrity to help them bridge the gap between knowledge and ambiguity.

When a manager hears a group suggesting that a specific individual would have good advice for an ambiguous decision, that person is worth viewing as a hidden leader. The leader's integrity means that the situation will be considered carefully. The hidden leader will give an honest opinion about what is important to know and what can be ignored. Because hidden leaders are secure in their ethical codes, they can manage ambiguity. They know they are doing their best, and they trust their ethics to carry them over potentially dangerous ground.

Hidden leaders with visible integrity think about more than their own needs and concerns. Because they adhere to a strong code of ethics, they think about the impact of actions on others. Faced with the opportunity to help, hidden leaders choose to support others' development, careers, and decisions that improve the situation for the largest number of people.

These hidden leaders are often the ones others suggest newly hired employees talk to about working successfully within the company. When people struggle with their positions and want a third-party opinion of their skills, they often go to these hidden leaders for advice. Employees caught in a spiral of conflict with a group or individual also often ask these leaders for help. They may ask about how they can successfully handle others' anger issues, power struggles, or apparent destructive behaviors. In all of these situations, hidden leaders are seen as appropriate resources because everyone knows they will tell the truth, even if it isn't what the person seeking advice really wants to hear. They know the leader will be fair and will couch negative feedback in a way that makes it easy to accept and work with. They also know that the hidden leader will strive to maintain an overarching view that fairly considers everyone's needs in the situation.

Those without this strong sense of fairness and integrity may appear to be helpful, but they might work behind the scenes to derail others' achievements or progress in a career or project. These are the secret tellers, backbiters, and problem originators in an organization. They are often described as having hidden agendas or motivations for their actions. They are looking out for themselves. Most people in the organization know who these people are, but others may be blinded by personal relationships or a lack of awareness or exposure. A wide-ranging evaluation of people who seem to have integrity to some, but are mistrusted by others, may uncover the discrepancies.

When people feel the support of hidden leaders, on the other hand, they trust those leaders fully. Managers will hear about recommendations made by a specific person, or notice individuals asking that person's advice on how to advance in the organization or improve skills and abilities. That person is the hidden leader who is open about helping everyone progress, for the benefit of each person, the organization, and the leader as well.

Early business organizations were structured by function. Few employees crossed the lines between functions to work with or interact with others. Today, that structural bias has changed. Innovative companies create cross-functional teams to develop products, organize systems, and solve problems. New structural systems are emerging that are flatter, meaning people with very different skills work together and have the same positional influence. Whether an organization has chosen to eliminate levels of management or several firms are working together virtually for short-term projects, more and more employees must work across functional boundaries and gain the respect of people in other fields and specialties.

For some people, this transition is difficult. Many people don't bother to understand others' work challenges and contributions and tend to think of their own functions as the sole anchors of a company's achievements.

But as you know, every function contributes to the success of an organization. Building bridges between functions so people understand how and what each one contributes is a major challenge. These bridges can mean the difference between reacting and innovating.

Hidden leaders naturally cross these functional boundaries, both in person and by reputation, because their integrity assumes that everyone is working toward the success of the company. They project their integrity on others. When they work with other functions, they ask questions to understand how that person or department fits into the entire structure that is the organization. They credit others for having expertise and trust that others speak the truth, unless proven otherwise.

One midlevel product manager we know was frustrated by his company's information technology (IT) department. The manager needed to enable a client company to access data stored on his company's servers. IT refused to allow this. In a cross-functional meeting to resolve the problem, the manager met one of the frontline programmers.

The meeting didn't resolve the issue, but the programmer, who was a hidden leader, took the initiative to talk in detail with the product manager. He learned why client companies needed to access certain company information behind the firewall, and he educated the project manager about the challenges of enabling such access to people outside of the company. During the conversation, both the product manager and the programmer realized the negative customer experience that would result if access created a data security breach. With this understanding, the hidden leader was able to work with customer-facing staff and internal IT colleagues to provide the critical data without allowing live access past digital security measures.

When colleagues in one function refer a problem or a challenge to someone in another function, it is possible that other person is a hidden leader. Through the leader's relationships and integrity as a person, the leader's reputation has seeped out of the functional area. People known across an organization—whether for honesty, integrity, ingenuity, or collaboration—

are often the hidden leaders who are truly concerned with others' success as well as their own.

WORKSHEET: IDENTIFY INTEGRITY

Use the worksheet below to help identify potential hidden leaders who demonstrate integrity in your organization. Answer each question without too much thought. You will remember the hidden leaders you've unknowingly interacted with or heard about. The online worksheet enables you to print or share your results.

bit.ly/GFJUpm

Answer this question...	By identifying a specific person
(Answer by identifying the first person who comes to mind.)	(Write a function or job title if you wish to protect the person's identity.)
A work team is stuck with a process problem. Who would its members ask outside of the team for help?	
A project faces a potential conflict of interest. Who raised the issue in the first place to the project team?	
When your team must make a decision without all the facts, to whom do the members go for advice?	
Who in your work group will dependably make decisions or act to address a problem?	
Who in your work group would you ask to identify someone who might be good for a specific role or project?	
Who in your organization is known for honesty? Collaboration? Ingenuity?	
If you wanted to understand what someone in another function does, who might you ask in your company?	
Who did you name most often?	

HOW CAN YOU SUPPORT INTEGRITY?

We don't pretend that we have the keys to affecting people's ethics in adulthood. Hopefully, your organization looks for and hires people who are moral and ethical in general. You begin with people whose values are consistent with the stated ones of the company.

However, courage and consistency in behaving with integrity can be encouraged or discouraged by co-workers, supervisors, and managers. Company structures and organizational responses can discourage people's ability to show integrity. They can make it difficult for employees to maintain moral positions contrary to demands of the organization. Such company structures and responses are especially influential when they organically conflict with the company's stated values.

For hidden leaders around you to thrive, you must support and show integrity in acting in accordance with your company's values, even if that integrity creates uncomfortable situations or challenging confrontations. Support emerges from people in positions of situational power who also display integrity: team leaders, supervisors, managers, and executives. In any organization, these are the people who initiate the culture that others will follow.

It is especially important that positional leaders show strong support when hidden leaders demonstrate integrity. We believe that this support takes three important forms: responding positively to integrity, incorporating integrity into the culture, and showing integrity yourself when it counts most: facing ethical dilemmas.

Integrity that is easy to engage is usually perceived as an obvious behavior. Management's response to difficult situations makes the biggest difference in a hidden leader's willingness to take a visible and ethical stand. When you as a manager see a hidden leader demonstrating integrity, especially in the face of rejection, it is important that you respond positively.

How do you know a difficult situation involves a hidden leader's integrity? This is the manager's challenge. Integrity emerges when others suggest processes or approaches that cross the line between honest and dishonest actions, and the hidden leader points out the dishonesty. It shows when people speak ill of someone in the room or not in the room, customer or otherwise, and the hidden leader objects. Sometimes it appears as conflict, as when a hidden leader refuses to adhere to a plan because it goes against the company's stated values. Similar conflicts emerge when the hidden leader sees actions that contradict market requirements or legal restrictions. Integrity can also arise when abusive behavior or speech is aimed at someone who cannot defend himself, for whatever reasons, and the hidden leader comes to that person's defense.

In these and other situations, your first responsibility is to determine if there are underlying causes for the conflict. If the conflict is based on personal issues unrelated to the problem, it is your responsibility to stop the conflict and help the people involved uncover whatever hidden agendas are driving problems. Knowledge of the people involved and the overall situation will help in that determination.

If, however, no hidden agendas emerge and a hidden leader truly is exhibiting integrity, you must support the leader's position, verbally and visibly. If conflict or abusive behavior is happening, first stop the conversation and ask people to take a few moments before continuing. Then, after acknowledging the hidden leader's courage in bringing up the issue, ask the group to discuss the situation and any ethical dilemmas raised.

A hidden leader might also demonstrate integrity by speaking to you privately to point out ethical lapses or dilemmas she is facing on the job. When this happens, support the leader by listening and addressing the situation. Others may have to be involved in the conversation later. Commend the leader when she has the courage to raise issues that affect the company and the customer.

Acknowledging integrity and acting to resolve the situation are excellent support mechanisms for hidden leaders. Rewarding integrity is a third supportive element. Rewards can be public acknowledgments, new assignments, or engaging the leader in the solution. By embracing the integrity of hidden leaders and not avoiding or hiding the issues, you best support the leader's courage and ability to continue to show integrity.

For example, Chuck, a division manager in a large insurance company, hired Linda, a technical writer, to help complete a product manual for insurance agents. Linda's employee status was LTE—limited-term employee. Her position would end as soon as she completed the assignment.

Different managers were responsible for each product, so Linda began by developing a work plan calling for a series of interviews with appropriate managers. After she got approval from Chuck, she began conducting the interviews. As she worked, one name came up several times—Nancy in the project management department. Linda learned that managers who hire LTE staff were required to work with the project management department to ensure that projects were completed on time and on budget. Chuck had never contacted anyone in that department.

This new information put Linda in an awkward position. Had Chuck neglected to involve project management when he hired her? Or was he trying to avoid oversight of his project for some reason? Unfamiliar with the culture of this workplace, Linda suspected that messy office politics were behind the situation.

Linda called Chuck before continuing her work. She said that she had learned that working with the project management department was a requirement for LTE managers and staff and that she felt uneasy going any further until the department was involved. Doing this was a risk for Linda: Calling attention to this issue could upset Chuck and put Linda's contract at risk.

Chuck did what a positional leader should do when he sees integrity. He thanked Linda for telling him. He agreed that Nancy should manage the project, and offered to contact her about Linda's work and deadlines. He would arrange for Linda to report to Nancy on schedule and budget matters while continuing to work with him and his team about the content of the manual.

"I apologize for not getting project management involved from the start," Chuck said. "This is the first time I've worked with an LTE, and I wasn't aware of the procedure." He thanked Linda again and assured her that she had acted appropriately.

Linda had behaved with integrity in a challenging situation. There was nothing insidious about Chuck's oversight, and he recognized and appreciated the intent of Linda's approach.

Ethical dilemmas are inevitable in any company trying to succeed. In organizations that support integrity, you can best handle these dilemmas in ways that support the company's ethics and values. Further, do not hesitate to discuss these dilemmas and the ethical management of them. In other words, support integrity by showing integrity, especially in the face of unpleasant behaviors, conflicts, and challenges.

Of course, you can show integrity only insofar as upper management does the same. If the executive suite encourages and rewards success-at-any-price behaviors, the entire culture will become ethically challenged. Those employees who do pride themselves on their integrity soon leave, which strengthens the dysfunctional culture. If you find yourself in a culture at odds with your personal integrity, you may want to look for another organization more attuned to your sense of right and wrong.

However, in many situations, ethical dilemmas emerge because the executive suite sets conflicting goals for the organization. For example, a salesperson may fudge reports to meet stated sales goals although knowing that the customer has not truly decided to buy. Given the salesperson's need to meet the goals or face a manager's ire (anticipated instead of the help needed to uncover why goals are not being met), this type of false reporting can be expected.

You can help by posing these conflicts to executives and asking them for guidance setting and supporting realistic priorities. You can also identify unintended consequences of certain success measures and ensure that the executive suite knows what is happening on the front lines. The classic example of this is a call center dedicated to customer service that measures (and rewards with bonuses) those workers who handle high call volumes. Without an added measure of customer service quality, no manager should expect people on the phones to value customer service.

A more critical example involves companies that profess safety as a high value but avoid answering questions about priorities from managers, supervisors, and employees when deadlines push. By evading a clear answer, executives undercut their stated value of safety because no one on the front lines truly believes management cares. They also undermine productivity: Given the choice between dangerous behaviors or productivity, supervisors and workers are unsure how to proceed. The result can be work slowdowns, confusion, or in the worst cases, employee injury.

By showing integrity when addressing these common challenges—as opposed to blaming others for the problems—you act as a role model for others. The courage and strength to do so will be rewarded by support from employees who will also address these challenges and dilemmas instead of ignoring them.

While most people believe they have strong ethical codes, many face situations in which adhering to those codes is a slippery slope. This may be because of conflicting requests or unclear assignments. You can help eliminate these challenges by consistently referring to the value promise of the company and emphasizing that success means success for all.

For example, a project manager with integrity may want to meet customer demands. But when those demands erode the company's profit margins or eat into the project manager's ability to help other customers, it's time to stop the slide. An ethical manager will point out that the customer and the company must succeed. If you can spot these situations before they occur, or offer reminders of what is important overall, you help integrate integrity into employees' daily thinking processes.

You can also talk about integrity when meeting with staff or peers. Raising the importance of what integrity means for the company reminds people of what constitutes ethical conduct. Proactive, regular discussions focus people on integrity and ethical behaviors and reinforce the organization's values.

By discussing integrity before it emerges as part of an issue or conflict, you help build a stronger code of ethics. Employees who can quote a manager's ongoing concern for integrity feel supported when they face dilemmas on their own.

DOES YOUR CULTURE SUPPORT INTEGRITY?

It is one thing for an organization to employ people who demonstrate integrity. It is another thing for an organization's culture to support that integrity.

Cultures supportive of integrity create environments that appreciate, recognize, and reward behaviors that are consistent with their values. This becomes obvious when ethical dilemmas emerge. In these situations, a culture's integrity is on display. Ongoing support for integrity is less obvious, though just as important, during everyday, sometimes-mundane actions of an organization's individuals. This daily support for integrity illustrates a culture's true commitment to integrity.

You can determine if your culture supports integrity by paying attention to everyday efforts and results. Does your company regularly deliver on its promises to customers? Are commitments met? Do people consistently act in the best interests of the enterprise, the customer, company stakeholders, and employees? Do workers get honest feedback about how they might improve performance? Are conversations genuine and productive in the face of conflicts? Do people believe they have contributed significantly to the organization? A company culture that can answer "yes" to all of these questions has aligned its actions with its integrity. For these things to be routine and usual, surrounding influences must clearly reinforce people who act in line with their integrity. People must be confident that the culture is on their side in terms of professional career and personal safety.

Organizations that demonstrate integrity enable people to create results while being consistent and reliable. This visible integrity is not just about character; it is also about capability. One of its clearest demonstrations is the ability to deliver on promises. That goes for individuals and organizations alike. When an organization's culture stresses accountability for actions, behaves in accordance with the values of the business, and establishes a safe environment for speaking the truth (especially when the truth is unpopular), it makes its integrity clearly visible.

Unfortunately, many hidden leaders find themselves in a company culture that does not support their demonstrated integrity. Sometimes these leaders are hired before their personal leadership traits have developed. Other times their integrity emerges because they see the damage that a toxic culture lacking integrity imposes on people and companies.

However they find themselves in nonsupportive organizations, hidden leaders are often punished when they demonstrate integrity. While some may hang on for longer periods of time, many will leave—or be asked to leave.

In psychology, it is a truism of family structures that if one member of the family changes the way he interacts within the family, one of two things will happen: The family, too, will change and adapt, or the changing person will be rejected from the family as a whole. The same is true in toxic or dysfunctional organizational cultures. When hidden leaders challenge the status quo, especially around integrity and ethics, either the organization shatters its old ways of doing things and transforms, person by person, or the hidden leader is fired—or quits.

For example, in one consulting project, our charter was to gather information about needed supervisory skills in a Bay Area tech company that was past its initial start-up stage. While the culture of the company was friendly and forward thinking in terms of its products, it was also largely male and white.

One frontline supervisor, a middle-aged woman, was in our opinion a highly qualified hidden leader: She was creative, experienced, and brave enough to say what was in everyone's minds in all types of meetings. She didn't grate when she spoke the truth and was able to couch her comments in terms everyone could understand. She also was fantastic at asking questions to help understand other people's positions and uncover any holes in their logic or thinking.

In a meeting with her manager, this hidden leader, who was white, mentioned that the company might review its hiring practices. She pointed out that they were in the middle of San Francisco, and no one in management was of Asian or African American descent. The only woman executive was the vice president of sales. But several salespeople had complained to this hidden leader that morale in sales was very low, largely because of their executive's perceived dishonesty. This leader wondered aloud to her manager when hiring diversity was going to be made a priority, since the customer base was very diverse.

The hidden leader's manager listened and said little about her comments. We were surprised, however, that in a few months, when the company faced layoffs because of lagging sales, this hidden leader was one of the first employees to be let go. Obviously, this culture was not open to internal questions about upper management's approach to employees, and it released a powerful figure who might have helped it reverse falling sales statistics.

You can spot if your organization is hurting itself by rejecting hidden leaders when it would benefit culturally and financially from listening to them instead. At that point, you also have a choice: Support the hidden leader by challenging the status quo, too, or leave the organization to join a culture that more closely matches your personal code of ethics and integrity.

Within cultures where the organization's morality conflicts with a hidden leader's individual ethical code, there will be conflict. The hidden leader will be the Cassandra, the person warning the organization that things are not all well and disaster is coming. In company cultures where the moral approach is to listen to others and evaluate situations objectively, these warnings may be heeded. In cultures where the individual doesn't matter—and sometimes honesty or collaboration don't matter either—the person will be ignored at the least or punished by demotion or removal.

If you listen closely, you can tell if your company culture supports or represses ethical questions by hidden leaders. When a team is about to do something wrong for the organization or customer, does someone say, "Oh, it doesn't matter"? When someone suggests a downright unlawful act, does the group accede silently without saying anything? When a hidden leader does point out an unethical decision, is that person commended—or fired?

All organizational cultures end up with the people they deserve—that is, the people who embody the culture's moral code, for good or bad. When a hidden leader doesn't fit, the group usually rejects the leader. By noticing which people the culture rejects, through firing or ignoring, you will learn a lot about your culture's moral and ethical code. If you see your organizational culture consistently acting against sustainable ethical and moral long-term interests, or the interests of its customers, stakeholders, and employees, it may be time to move on.

It's easy to be consistent when everyone agrees. When people offer opposing ideas, solutions, and decisions, consistency is more difficult to maintain. In healthy organizations, these conflicts are resolved by finding new solutions or making new decisions that incorporate the fundamental ethics of those involved and are best for the organization and its customers, stakeholders, and employees. In dysfunctional or toxic organizations, the solution to conflict is often asking individuals to abandon their beliefs and moral judgments.

Consistency doesn't mean obstinacy. Hidden leaders depend on their code of ethics to help them make decisions. Because these codes are broad based and include the well-being of everyone in the situation, they enable hidden leaders to adjust their views and remain true to their ethics while adjusting the "how" of an action. Those who maintain consistency and are inflexible in light of others' needs are not hidden leaders: They are simply stubborn.

True hidden leaders often step back when conflict arises. They use their relational skills to communicate their own points of view and ask others to clearly state their opinions. Then hidden leaders tend to find common ground that enables everyone to remain true to their fundamental beliefs and ethics.

When hidden leaders act this way in a dysfunctional culture, you may see them labeled as troublemakers or meddlers. Others may pressure them to let go of their points "just this time" and oppose them when the same issues arise again and again over time. When you see an individual constantly in conflict who states fundamental ethical beliefs as the source of the problem, you would be well served to investigate this person and situation.

There are, of course, troublemakers and meddlers who simply want attention or want to be right; your research will have to uncover those. But when so-called troublemakers have a strong ethical code and present their argument in a way that would promote the interests of the company, you have found a hidden leader who could help transform that culture into a more healthy and successful organization.

One of the most difficult aspects of demonstrating integrity is the courage to do so in conflict situations. We have already identified this characteristic as one of the foundations of the hidden leader. But how a specific culture responds to a hidden leader's courageous acts reveals more about the culture than the hidden leader.

When a culture is truly open to the contributions of all employees, the courage to show integrity is rewarded. People listen to hidden leaders who are speaking out and act to support the leader's observations. Others acknowledge a hidden leader's integrity. These companies find ways to resolve issues or solve problems when hidden leaders point out actions that contradict the organization's own ethical position.

In company cultures with hidden agendas—where an actual goal (usually of increasing profits) is in conflict with a stated goal (such as safety or customer service)—the courage to demonstrate integrity is often punished. Such courage can also earn a hidden leader the reputation as a troublemaker or complainer. In extreme cases, when multiple hidden leaders display courage, it can prompt conflict between management and employees.

We have seen this especially in sectors like manufacturing, where some work is potentially physically dangerous. If management verbalizes the importance of safety but finances only productivity (say by not providing sufficient workers on an assembly line), hidden leaders will speak up and build support from others. The result can be dangerous to the productivity of the company as a whole and does not build trust between those doing the dangerous work and their managers.

Punishment can be subtle in situations where hidden leaders show the courage to act. For example, in a team meeting, a hidden leader might question how well customers will be served by a specific change in product marketing or pricing. If you hear no discussion about these comments, or others simply ignore them or deem them to be irrelevant, you may be working in a culture with hidden agendas. Other elements may be at play, but when these comments pass unmanaged, it is wise to investigate further.

Sometimes punishment for raising ethical issues is more intense than simply being ignored or made irrelevant. Hidden leaders may have their careers derailed. They may see important projects assigned to others or their contributions to fundamental decisions minimized. If you see a potential hidden leader marginalized, wonder about the source of this treatment. Are there other agendas besides the public ones under which everyone is working? Do some individuals wield more power behind the scenes, noticeably those who are not liked or admired within the organization?

When a culture is functioning well, it takes courage to raise issues that may go against the opinions of others. In dysfunctional cultures, this courage is punished, so hidden leaders may refrain from showing integrity. In most cases, when they can, they leave (or are asked to leave) to find a culture that appreciates their abilities to remain ethical and honest even in difficult situations.

WHAT CAN YOU DO TO ENABLE CULTURAL INTEGRITY?

Ultimately, how management creates and sustains a company's cultural environment is what enables integrity. As we stated earlier, this is more than not lying, stealing, or cheating. It also means creating a culture that encourages people to say the same things up and down the established chain of command. Cultures with integrity discourage employees from discussing one thing privately and espousing something else publicly. They also reject personal agendas that are not in line with the interests of the organization. Enabling integrity as a culture is less about rules and more about how people behave on a consistent basis.

When we work with companies to improve or change elements of their culture, one of the most frequent focus areas is values and how they are modeled. While it is fundamental for a company to promote its values to its employees, it is critical that positional leaders of the organization champion those values in their daily decisions. Hidden leaders can help create ethical cultures because their behaviors are driven by their personal ethical codes. Since organizational culture reflects the underlying beliefs that drive behavior, others look to hidden leaders as the models for these beliefs.

You can promote cultural values in your organization by taking them seriously. Look for ways to link these values to decisions and comments you make. Help others see connections to values. Further, speak up yourself when you see your company's values exploited for the wrong reasons, or contradicted by decisions, actions, and pronouncements.

Many daily decisions or actions made within organizations are not necessarily dealing with right or wrong. Sometimes people must choose between two ethical alternatives. In these cases, a culture that supports the organization's values creates an environment that enables people to make good decisions. By "good" we mean effective, productive, and positive decisions that lead to a better future for the company, its people, and its customers. Making and keeping commitments, being transparent about decisions, and demonstrating consistency are the kinds of good behaviors that reinforce the integrity of an organization. They help establish cultures that support integrity.

Keeping verbal and contractual commitments builds credibility and trust in organizations and people. When this accountability is expected, it reinforces integrity as a core value of the organization. Institutional reliability creates an atmosphere where people know they can depend on others to do their parts.

For example, we were interviewing a team of engineers in a large telecommunications firm about the culture of the organization. During the conversation, one of the participants described how team members "played with a no-look pass." This basketball reference, describing how one player confidently lobs the ball toward a teammate while looking in another direction, was telling. It implied that all team members could be counted on to do their parts.

This team's feeling of integrity was palpable. It was clear team members trusted one another to make good choices and perform at high levels. This confidence emerged not from blind trust, but because team members had a record of keeping commitments. They personified the values of the organization in integrity that showed.

Transparency in decision making allows people to see explicitly the rationale for choices and directions. Visibility about why decisions are made creates an environment that encourages open discussion and an exchange of ideas. This is particularly valuable when trying to increase employee engagement, which many of our clients express as an important objective. For example, when companies openly share financial information as an underpinning of corporate goals, it demonstrates a culture where trust and integrity is prized. This encourages a deeper level of involvement from those in the organization.

Consistency in decisions, approaches, and behaviors also supports integrity. When workers can count on you to respond consistently, it creates a sense of ease. This sense is not a lack of variety in the negative sense. It is an ease born of trust that you will act in the best interests of all involved.

Each of these factors—keeping commitments, consistency, and transparency—underpin a culture of integrity. They are also factors that influence an organization's ability to deliver high performance and value to its customers.

Many times, we have seen perfectly ethical people in an organization do things that didn't make sense for the company, the customer, or other stakeholders. It wasn't that the culture was unethical; it was that certain structures were in place that actually rewarded people for doing the wrong thing. In these situations, hidden leaders are unlikely to raise issues and concerns, because the structures around them are created and condoned by management.

In sales, we see this sort of structural conflict regularly. Annually, a company's most successful salespeople are often "rewarded" by being assigned ever-higher quotas. These quotas are measured monthly or quarterly, although a rapid sales cycle for a company's critical product is many months long. We have seen many companies that neglect to measure any interim steps, forcing salespeople to either hide upcoming sales until they need the numbers or stuff poor prospects into the pipeline. In our opinion, it isn't that these salespeople necessarily lack integrity; it's that the very structure of how salespeople are measured and managed promotes questionable reporting.

Decades ago, America's train companies were in trouble. Trucking had not yet developed as an obvious partner to train transportation, and no train organization in the country was making a profit. It looked like moving products by train was on the way out.

One company, desperate to improve its productivity, created a simple rule for its engine shops, which repaired the huge diesel engines that made the railroad run. No one engine could be in a shop for more than three days. The intent was that the shops would focus on getting the engines up and running again.

The result was, sadly, hilarious: Caught with a badly damaged engine, and measured for success only in terms of moving engines out, a general manager simply told the shop manager to hitch the unrepairable-in-three-days engine to a train that was headed for someone else's region. The result: The company's most badly damaged engines were dragged around the country for years, unrepaired.

With no general manager measured on the impact he or she might have on other regions, but each one rewarded for getting those engines out on time, the GMs were "successful," as the company lost the use of some of its most important property—the engines that ran the business. Executives and managers throughout a company need to evaluate measurement systems carefully for unintended consequences like these. For better or worse, it is our experience that what is measured gets done, although what gets done may, at heart, damage the company's bottom line.

Perhaps we are too optimistic, but we believe most people want to do the right thing. But to expect a hidden leader to stand up to the entire structure of a company and push back against management's measurement rules in order to do the right thing is Pollyanna thinking at its worst. To ensure a strong, ethical culture from the beginning, look at potential unintended consequences of the measurement system within your organization. Communicate negative consequences to your management. In most cases, you will find that the C-level did not intend for these to emerge in the quest for effective measurement.

CAN YOU TEACH INTEGRITY?

A person's integrity develops early in life. Once formed, it is difficult to alter, change, or improve a person's integrity or ethical position. It becomes part of each person's individual psychology or self-identity.[2]

We do not believe integrity can be taught in the organizational environment. It can be supported with behaviors congruent with company values. Alternatively, individuals' integrity can be undermined with aggressive verbal attacks, a lack of support, and "political" actions within an organization.

We believe that many people work from a base of integrity, whether it shows or not. We see employees exhibit integrity regularly. Not all of them, however, are hidden leaders. This doesn't mean they are not valuable to your organization. People with integrity are an important part of a company's success. The more that integrity can be incorporated, from the top down, into an organization's culture, supported, and rewarded, the better that company's employees will be able to bond, engage, and succeed.

If you see people who you believe have shown integrity leaving your company because they have been admonished or called troublemakers, or simply feel they are in the wrong environment, it may be time to take stock of how your organization and its leaders are embodying integrity. The following assessment may help you determine if you are working for an organization with integrity. Your own experience is also valuable. Is it easy to raise troublesome issues with management? Do you feel supported when you raise issues to people in powerful positions? Are you confident that the stated values of your organization truly drive decision making at the highest levels?

On the other hand, if you see hidden leaders who show integrity and are neither punished nor rewarded, it may mean your company has integrity but management is not aware of the important role it can play in your company's success. By pointing out ways to support people with integrity, you can help change the culture to one that is open, consistent with its values, and courageous enough to face the challenges of innovation and the marketplace.

WORKSHEET: EVALUATE YOUR COMPANY'S INTEGRITY

While most people believe they have integrity, their actions may indicate that their code of ethics is not strong or consistent, or they lack courage to speak truth during conflict or in difficult situations. The same is true of organizational cultures. How peers and executives respond to hidden leaders' visible integrity illustrates the company's level of integrity. Use the statements below to assess how well your company supports hidden leaders and their integrity. Access the worksheet online for an automatic score.

bit.ly/1gg382X

Statement	Frequency (1=Never, 5=Always)				
C-level executives stress the importance of integrity as part of their regular communications.	1	2	3	4	5
Your company's stated values reflect strong ethical concepts.	1	2	3	4	5
Actions by executives, managers, and supervisors consistently reflect the stated values of the organization.	1	2	3	4	5
When employees or peers point out ethical dilemmas, others listen and use the comments as the basis for discussion.	1	2	3	4	5
When employees question processes or actions based on their inconsistency with the company's values, employees are rewarded or commended by someone in management.	1	2	3	4	5
In ambiguous situations, the company's leaders refer to the stated values as a means of determining action.	1	2	3	4	5
People in general commend, reward, or mention employees who get excellent work done.	1	2	3	4	5
Managers and supervisors credit the people they manage for successful results.	1	2	3	4	5
Most people speak openly about issues and concerns.	1	2	3	4	5
People talk to each other about conflicts instead of going behind the scenes to get others to deal with the issue.	1	2	3	4	5
People who challenge the status quo remain with the organization for long periods of time.	1	2	3	4	5
Total Score (Higher score=More integrity)					

CHAPTER FOUR

Build Essential Relational Skills

Hidden leaders with strong relational leadership develop and use critical interpersonal skills whether or not they have been officially trained in them. The hidden leader's life experiences, combined with an interest in others, make these leaders more self-aware than nonleaders. This self-awareness emerges as compassion and empathy for other people. Hidden leaders are highly aware of their impact on people and conscious of their needs.

This is not to imply that those who lead through relationships have some innate gift that cannot be replicated. Anyone can develop these skills. Too often described as "soft" skills in the business world (in our view, a misnomer that minimizes their importance), these are critical skills that are distinct, specific, and eminently teachable.

While it is simple to define and identify relational leadership skills, it doesn't mean they are easy to learn. Simple, straightforward skills are often the most difficult to learn because they require a deep understanding of each aspect of the skill. Knowing how to best swing a golf club doesn't automatically translate into a good golf swing—as Scott can attest. Those who lead through relationships make interpersonal skills seem easy because they use the skills effectively. These skills are not complicated, but they require a deep foundation in empathy, compassion, and emotional health.

Given a baseline of interest in others, a hidden leader can learn these skills and integrate them into everyday performance easily. Teaching relational leadership skills to a hidden leader who shows other important characteristics of hidden leadership is a great investment.

THE SOURCE OF RELATIONAL LEADERSHIP

Hidden leaders who effectively lead through relationships often recognize their lack of positional leadership. They know they cannot depend on their role as a boss to influence others' actions. At bottom, though, the hidden leader's incentive to lead through relationships is not one of getting ahead or manipulating others well. It is based in the leader's appreciation of others and the knowledge that all work is completed with a team—whether or not the team actually gets the credit for the work.

These elements of relational leadership—valuing others, compassion, interpersonal skills, and open curiosity—translate into emotional maturity. Relational leaders are naturally emotionally healthy in the context of the job. This emotional maturity enables the self-awareness to empathize with others and use interpersonal skills as a way to develop real relationships, not just as a means of getting along.

Leading through relationships doesn't mean that each of the hidden leader's relationships needs to be a deep, enduring friendship. Some are exclusively based in the workplace, of course. In this context, effective relational leaders maintain connections with colleagues that are not just task focused or transactional in nature. They are true interpersonal relationships, based in an interest in people.

Throughout this discussion of relational leadership, we've mentioned authenticity, integrity, and honesty as key traits of the relational leader. This is the human aspect of hidden leadership: emotional maturity and intelligence.

Relational leadership is more than emotional intelligence, which refers to people's ability to manage their emotions. Leading through relationships, in our view, means hidden leaders manage their emotions well but also focus on the emotions of others by developing authentic relationships.

Like any other trait, emotions can be negative in the workplace. We have all seen the hysterical, angry, or demeaning leader who uses a position of authority to browbeat and berate people into performing. Such leaders get compliance, not commitment, and levels of productivity suffer, as our studies of those perceived as poor leaders show.

What about the positive side of emotions? Hidden leaders who are generous, optimistic, supportive, and encouraging tend to get commitment that goes far beyond compliance. They engage others in solving problems and fostering innovation.

There's more to relational leaders than a spate of positive emotions, though. Because hidden leaders are good at interpersonal skills, they are excellent at making emotional connections with others. Few things are more important to leadership.

An emotional connection is not being overtly emotional or indulging in wild displays of emotion. Rather, it is a human connection that goes beyond task, job, or output and creates a personal bond. The emotions synonymous with this connection are passion, enthusiasm, and energy— the kinds of emotions that often influence and motivate others.

Research for Scott's book *The Inspiring Leader*[1] clearly indicated the importance of leaders' abilities to make emotional connections. Of all of the leadership skills that correlated with the ability to inspire and motivate others, being able to make productive emotional connections ranked first. This was uncovered through a regression analysis of over twenty thousand leaders. The analysis studied the characteristics of leaders who ranked in the 90th percentile of those able to inspire others. The results showed that if leaders inspired and motivated those around them, odds are they easily made emotional connections.

Authenticity in interpersonal relationships must be the foundation of the interpersonal skills that build such relationships. This is an integral part of relational leadership for any hidden leader. One cannot fake emotional or human connections over the long term. The best actor will not be convincing forever if he truly is not interested in the other person. For the hidden leader who leads through relationships, the interest is ipso facto in the relationship itself.

The baseline of making an emotional connection is an honest interest in others, which is the same baseline for relational leadership as a whole. No one can fake this interest. But we have seen relational leaders do three critical things that help build emotional connections beyond basic relational skills.[2]

- ◘ **They pay attention to others.** With instant messaging, texting, and the constant buzz of smartphone connectivity, paying attention is becoming harder and harder to do. But those who lead through relationships focus on the people around them. This ability creates a sense of connection. There is no question about the positive effect on relationships when a leader is fully engaged with the person in front of him. On the other hand, incessantly checking for messages or multitasking while on the phone clearly communicate that the other person is not important. In most cases, hidden leaders make it a point to give others their undivided attention.

- ◘ **They make an effort to connect.** Hidden leaders reach out to others and engage them in discussions, involve them in projects, and solicit their ideas. Although not in a formal leadership role, the hidden leader includes others to foster collaboration and teamwork. This doesn't necessarily translate to being an extrovert. An effort from a quiet hidden leader is clearly noted since these introverted leaders limit their verbal contributions. It is the effort to connect that makes the difference.

- ◘ **They time conversations to coincide with their own positive moods.** No one can be totally positive at all times. For hidden leaders, reality intrudes with difficult moments. The difference for relational leaders who make emotional connections is that they wait to have difficult conversations until they are able emotionally.

We have all been around leaders who are effective at helping people embrace positive emotions. These leaders are excited about the prospect of success, and their enthusiasm and energy influence others. They infuse hope into individuals and teams and create confidence.

This transference of emotional energy isn't imaginary. Think about the last time one of your colleagues arrived at work angry about something. During your interactions with this person, could you feel tension? Perhaps you adopted a defensive posture, or became irritated yourself. The negativity from that experience may have put you in a lousy mood. Were you able to shrug it off easily afterwards, or did it continue to affect you until you got home that evening?

On the other hand, remember a time when a co-worker arrived happy and enthusiastic about work and life. How did those emotions affect your attitude and work? Did the positive energy continue to enhance your day? How did those emotions help you address challenges with the day's work? How much did you want to be around that person afterward?

Our experience working with individuals and teams is that our emotional states can be both positively and negatively affected by our colleagues' emotions. The more central a person is to our work role, the greater the effect of that person's emotions on us. When work colleagues are also friends, the power of their emotions is even stronger. Positively or negatively, the impact of an interaction with this person can extend to later conversations you have with others.

For hidden leaders, this emotional influence is a strength because they operate from positive points of view. With positive emotions, hidden leaders can create, influence, and build optimism, confidence, and excitement in their peers. Their enthusiasm is contagious. The effects can be felt at many levels of the organization. For most people, routinely interacting with hidden leaders who are passionate about their work and approach their jobs with enthusiasm is a positive experience. It enables some of that attitude to influence their approaches to work.

Peers of one hidden leader we know, an analyst for a financial services client, often commented to us, "When Shaun is in a meeting, it's always more productive and the energy is higher." They also said, "Shaun's positive approach toward solving problems sets the tone for all of us."

In our view, this explains the importance of hidden leaders' abilities to make emotional connections with colleagues. By connecting with many people throughout an organization, relational leaders can inspire positive emotional energy. The influence will not be as significant among those who don't consider themselves friends per se, and none of this suggests that people come to work and focus on making friends. But relational leaders, because of their interest in others, can inspire through their abilities to make emotional connections independent of traditional friendships.

Relational leadership is in play when a leader, positional or otherwise, is able to connect with people throughout an organization. Based in an interest in others, this ability to establish relationships is critical for hidden leaders. Relational leadership makes working with the hidden leader engaging. Emotional connections made transcend daily responsibilities and build loyalty, enthusiasm, and trust. These characteristics are important for positional leaders, too. For hidden leaders, they are essential, since these leaders cannot lean on any authority assigned by the organization. When people work with and for hidden leaders, they do so because of the relationships involved.

DEVELOPING ESSENTIAL RELATIONAL SKILLS

Hidden leaders consistently use a specific set of observable skills. For hidden leaders who lead through relationships, these skills are a natural outgrowth of their interest in and respect for people. They are face-to-face communication skills, transparent critical thinking, crediting others, honest and complete critiques, and effective conflict resolution.

While not all hidden leaders may exhibit these skills at the same levels of expertise, they do them well enough to create, build, and maintain relationships at many levels within an organization. Skills that are weak or missing can be developed through training, practice, feedback, and coaching. These skills can also be part of a complete performance development plan, which we will discuss more fully in Chapter 7.

Understanding the skills that build relationships is your first step in identifying and supporting hidden leaders who lead through relationships. In this chapter, we will examine what each of these skills entails and how to spot them at work.

Face-to-Face Communication Skills

Authentic relationships entail communicating one-on-one with people. We call these baseline skills face-to-face communications skills. We recognize that in today's virtual and digital world, "face-to-face" may sometimes mean "voice-to-voice" or "video-to-video." For our purposes, "face-to-face" means the fundamental methods two people use to communicate verbally and initiate, build, and maintain strong interpersonal relationships. These skills are verbal ones; they cannot be used to build connections between people via written communications, such as email.

Sharing Information

One of the first things people do in any relationship is share information. As relationships grow, the participants feel enough connection with the other person to share information that is more and more personal. This is a touchstone of a strong relationship. Sharing is also the foundation of feeling as if you are heard, which emerges from the use of three other face-to-face communication skills: clarifying, confirming, and acknowledging others.

The information one shares, in terms of detail, intent, and purpose, differs according to situation. How one shares effectively involves two very simple (yet not always easy to do) elements: saying *what* you want or mean and adding *why* you want or mean it.

- ◘ *What* you want or mean most often consists of objective facts and truths. The *what* can be the same for many people. For example, "I want to meet this deadline" means the same whether the speaker is a manager, supervisor, or frontline worker.

- ◘ *Why* the speaker wants to achieve the *what* is the differentiating element of sharing information. The *why* changes and has different depths of meaning for various individuals.

A manager might say, "I want to meet this deadline (*what*) because we've made a commitment to the customer—and we keep our commitments (*why*)." Someone working for that manager might say (in a different context), "I want to meet this deadline (*what*) because I'm being measured on my ability to manage my time effectively (*why*)." Each statement reflects an honest and important reason to meet the deadline, and each contains a different level of meaning for both speaker and listener. Both are valid.

Sharing information by detailing both what and why is important because it makes it easier for the listener to understand. It reduces confusion, sets out important parameters, and shows that the speaker is talking with the listener's needs in mind.

All good communicators think from the listener's point of view. These communicators, hidden leaders among them, recognize that trust builds when people are not surprised. Saying both what and why reduces the element of surprise and helps others understand the underlying reasons for any statement.

Clarifying and Confirming

When people encounter a hidden leader who leads through relationships, they often say something like, "She is a great listener—that's why it's easy to communicate with her." But our experience working with thousands of leaders to develop this skill demonstrates that being a good listener is not just hearing the other person. It is about asking questions to *clarify* and *confirm* what the listener has heard.

Because hidden leaders use these skills appropriately and effectively, to the listener it seems that the leader hasn't spoken at all. The leader has simply been able to understand the speaker's concerns accurately, which feels to the speaker like good listening.

Like all face-to-face skills, clarifying and confirming are easy to describe. Clarifying is asking questions to see *if* one understands what the speaker has said. Confirming entails asking questions that prove *that* one understands what the speaker has said. In practice, these skills are both critical. Sometimes they are difficult to do well.

For example, clarifying questions pose queries that ask for more information:

- Are you saying that the deadline is impossible to meet, given the existing process?

- What makes you think we can't meet this deadline?

- What process steps are slowing us down?

Confirming questions may take some of the very same information, but they indicate that the listener has heard the information correctly.

- So you think we cannot meet this deadline, right?

- You are saying it is the process that is holding us up, correct?

- It sounds like you think quality-control steps will prevent us from meeting the deadline, right?

Each of the two types of questions poses specific challenges when it comes to using them effectively.

- Clarifying questions are sometimes difficult to imagine because we do not notice our own assumptions; these may block our awareness that we do not know all of the pertinent facts. (Another important relational skill, transparent critical thinking, helps address this difficulty, as we will discuss later.)

- Confirming questions can be hard because truly confirming is more than restating exactly what the other person said. Effective confirming questions restate what the other person said in our own words, so we can truly test our understanding.

How important are clarifying and confirming? Done well, these two listening skills eliminate confusion, misunderstandings, and concerns that cost organizations millions of dollars on a daily basis. Misheard assignments, missed deadlines, wrong decisions, and emerging conflicts can be averted when people clarify and confirm as they listen. Hidden leaders use these skills well because they know that being able to truly hear what a person says is not only an important part of a relationships but also a critical component of productivity, innovation, and effectiveness in a company. In short, it makes life easier for all.

Acknowledging Others

Acknowledgment doesn't mean agreement. Communication is exchanging ideas and information between two people or among parties. If we are effectively sharing information and clarifying and confirming, inevitably some information exchanged will not be to our liking. Ignoring or disagreeing with that information will not help build a relationship.

Hidden leaders know that when they hear information or ideas with which they do not agree, expressing just disagreement can be harmful. By acknowledging the other person's contribution of that idea or information, the disagreement will not negatively affect the relationship. By then exploring the conflicting piece of information through transparent critical thinking, hidden leaders can actually avert conflict and use the information to help build a mutual solution.

Acknowledging others is, like our other face-to-face skills, often difficult to do. Many people feel that acknowledging the other person's point as valid is the same as agreeing with that point. People's egos and fears drive this feeling, to the extent that they cannot acknowledge that the other person has made any point, much less a valid one. At that juncture, conflicts often arise.

Hidden leaders know that one can acknowledge without agreeing and still build trust in a relationship. They are confident enough in their own knowledge and beliefs—and sense of self-identity—that giving to others is not seen as taking away from the leaders. Sometimes people just need to be heard. They want their views acknowledged.

In many ways, acknowledging others is akin to confirming: It is expressing *that* one has heard the other person's contribution. The difference between the two is subtle:

- Confirming focuses on the listener's understanding. It entails asking or implying a question to ensure that the listener understands correctly.

◘ Acknowledging focuses on the speaker's contribution. It is usually a statement that outlines the contribution and credits the speaker with raising valid information that is pertinent to the speaker or situation.

As with clarifying and confirming, people credit hidden leaders who acknowledge others as being "good listeners," although the skill itself entails speaking. And, as with other relational skills, hidden leaders acknowledge others authentically. They see value in the other person's contribution, even when it conflicts with their own ideas. This ability to operate from the other's point of view is a foundation of hidden leaders' relational skills and evident in their effective face-to-face communication.

Transparent Critical Thinking

Critical thinking is a sought-after business skill. Critical thinkers differentiate facts from assumptions, examine logical arguments, develop rational conclusions, and synthesize solutions. They can remove emotional or irrational arguments from a discussion. Good critical thinkers extend the process to help others through effective questioning, asking about other people's assumptions, conclusions, and facts on which they are basing their arguments.

In our experience, hidden leaders are good critical thinkers. But they add an extra dimension to their critical thinking: They make it transparent to the people around them.

Transparent critical thinking is the ability to make verbal connections for people between the facts or assumptions that support an argument and the conclusions or solutions. Transparent critical thinkers verbalize their thought process so others can see how they came to a conclusion or the rationale behind a solution. By making critical thinking transparent we do not mean thinking aloud. People who blurt out what they are thinking while they think it are not making their critical thinking transparent—they are simply sharing all of their thoughts as they occur. People who ramble between subjects or rehash or restate previous statements in a discussion are not making their thinking transparent either. They are making all of their thoughts verbal and, in many cases, boring or confusing people and wasting time.

The value of transparent critical thinking is that it makes public the facts, assumptions, logic, and synthesis of the hidden leader's thought process. It provides both the *what* and the *why*. If facts or assumptions are wrong, others in the conversation can point out the errors or question the assumptions. If the logic is based on a fallacy or inconsistency, others can determine how to fix the error. If a conclusion or solution does not logically result from its basis, or does not address other facts or assumptions critical to the situation, others are already informed. They can then either develop new solutions or alter the conclusion or solution so it does follow from the underlying facts.

Transparent critical thinking speeds a conversation. It provides the rationale and helps engage people in the thought process. It eliminates potential arguments based on erroneous "facts" or unknown assumptions. It builds on the creativity of those involved and results more often in strong, workable solutions that address all the elements involved.

Because transparent critical thinking automatically involves others, it also builds relationships and trust. Hidden leaders who make their critical thinking transparent trust the listeners, and the listeners are confident that there not hidden agendas at work in the situation. The result is not only better thinking. Transparent critical thinking deepens relationships within the group, both between group members and the hidden leader, and among the group members as a whole.

Crediting Others

Hidden leaders know that it is rare for a great accomplishment to be achieved by one person in a vacuum. Multiple contributors, at many levels, are involved in a success. Hidden leaders not only pay attention to the potentially unsung contributors to success, they make sure they give them public credit for their contributions.

This willingness to credit others' contributions strengthens relationships deeply. In many corporate cultures, managers and supervisors assume that if they haven't criticized a worker, the worker should somehow know the exact things he or she is doing well. The hidden leader, on the other hand, identifies specific contributions and tells others about the person's work. This builds a relationship between the hidden leader and the contributor because the person feels appreciated.

Being noticed, seen, and appreciated is a great basis for relationships in any context. For hidden leaders, it stems from a natural drive to credit others based on an authentic appreciation of their contributions. This drive emerges both in public (meetings and conversations where many are present) and private (mentioning excellence to supervisors and managers in one-on-one conversations).

To some people, crediting others seems to detract from the speaker's own reputation. Hidden leaders know that crediting others only builds their own reputations as honest, appreciative, and alert co-workers. It also helps the hidden leader solidify relationships and build loyalty.

Honest and Complete Critiques

Success and productivity depend on people being effective at their work. Hidden leaders believe that most people do their best, but they also know that people make mistakes. Because they truly value relationships, hidden leaders want to help others improve their performance however possible. One of the tools hidden leaders use to help others is to provide honest and complete critiques of actions, behaviors, or work products.

Hidden leaders' honest and complete critiques use a simple structure that is designed to help the other person, not harm. Honest and complete critiques:

- **Focus on the content.** Hidden leaders take care to point out facts or behaviors relative to the situation, both effective and ineffective. They do not make the critique of the person but of the person's actions.

- **Maintain the person's value.** Hidden leaders disconnect the person's inherent value from the value of the ineffective action or observed behavior.

◻ **Build with information.** Hidden leaders propose adjustments based on information, not emotional judgments or responses.

Hidden leaders know when to provide honest and complete critiques. In general, they look for private venues to discuss how a person could improve skills or behaviors in a specific situation. Meetings, group conversations, and similar situations are not good times for critiques. Of course, the hidden leader does not critique someone's actions or behavior when that person is not in the room to hear.

Yet the hidden leader doesn't shy away from honest and complete critiques in one-on-one situations. Because the hidden leader focuses on the content, the person's personality or unrelated behaviors are not mentioned. By maintaining the person's value as a person, no matter what error of judgment occurred, the hidden leader helps the other person accept the content of the critique. Any suggestions for change are built on information, whether from the hidden leader's technical knowledge, personal experience, or observations of others.

The ability to provide honest and complete critiques makes hidden leaders valuable sounding boards. Because people feel the honesty and the intent of helping, relationships are strengthened and people are more likely to take the hidden leader's advice.

Effective Conflict Resolution

The best communicators cannot evade conflict all the time. Nor should conflict avoidance be a goal. Sometimes processes, goals, and opinions clash. These events can be productive if handled well: They can lead to innovations, creativity, and new ideas as each side cedes to the constrictions of the other. Some conflicts do not contribute anything to the overall good of the company. In the main, they can be personality clashes or struggles for power. The key to effective conflict resolution is in characterizing the kind of conflict and managing it appropriately.

Good conflicts—those of ideas, priorities, goals, and opinions—respond well to transparent critical thinking and logical, systematic approaches to solutions. Hidden leaders handle these situations well because they are confident in the power of methodical processes and rational conclusions. They also succeed at managing these conflicts because they trust that those involved have the good of the customer and the company at heart. We call these creative conflicts, because often the results or solutions that emerge are better than the two initial options combined.

In creative conflicts, hidden leaders use their communication skills to identify facts, assumptions, goals, and priorities among the parties involved. Then they search for ways to combine all the stated goals into one systematic solution. This ability to synthesize solutions from conflicting ideas makes hidden leaders the relational anchor points for people involved in the conflict. Hidden leaders also strive to triangulate conflicts: to separate them from the people involved and place them outside of specific relationships. This helps build consensus because when ideas conflict, the group is able to tackle the conflict separate from specific people within the group. With the problem outside of any one person, suddenly people can disagree without being disagreeable and challenge ideas instead of one another.

Damaging conflicts—the conflicts based on personality clashes or power struggles—are often more difficult to resolve. Hidden leaders try, using their strong relationship skills and transparent critical thinking, to help both sides come to terms.

A hidden leader we observed was working to help his investment company streamline key processes. One critical department was the mail room. Because this financial corporation worked 24/7 to adapt to worldwide markets, there were three shift supervisors in the mail room. The daytime supervisor worked the usual nine to five, while the evening supervisor worked until two in the morning, and a third supervisor took the all-night shift.

The challenge in this situation was the relationship between the night-shift supervisor and the daytime one. The problem was one of personalities. The night-shift supervisor was an older man who had worked with the company since its inception many years earlier. He was happy with his position: He felt he provided an important service, and the quality of his team's work was his primary focus. However, the day-shift supervisor was a management trainee who had just joined the company. She saw the mail room as a stepping-stone to something better. She felt she needed to do a good job, which entailed making sure any problems were resolved quickly.

The challenge came in the early morning handoff between the two supervisors. By 8 a.m., the night-shift supervisor was at the end of his day. He had to tell the incoming supervisor important information about work done during the night, and he was tired and ready to go home. But the day-shift supervisor, often late to the mail room because of other priorities, felt the information was not all that important. When she appeared significantly after 8 a.m., there was a verbal confrontation between the two.

In addition to this essential conflict, the two supervisors did not like each other personally. The older man thought the younger woman was irresponsible; the woman felt the man was stubborn and trying to make things hard for her.

Our hidden leader talked to both supervisors at length. (He was the only one in the organization who took the initiative to do so.) He discovered that there was important information one supervisor had to give to the other. He also found out that it was discrete information that was easy to quantify with a number.

The hidden leader knew that personality-wise, these two supervisors were not going to like each other. The leader also knew that a simple, new form, completed by the night supervisor and placed on the day supervisor's desk, would communicate the important information. The night supervisor could go home after his shift, and the day supervisor could see to her other responsibilities at her leisure, knowing the information she needed would be there.

This hidden leader was no efficiency expert or process consultant. But by talking with (and listening to) both people involved, he saw a damaging conflict and an opportunity to resolve it by changing a procedure. Both supervisors felt heard, both felt they were still in the right, and both felt their needs had been met. This hidden leader accomplished it all with the design of a simple, one-page form.

A damaging conflict is often based on emotional issues both related and unrelated to the situation. Even a hidden leader may not attempt to counsel people in such a situation. However, a hidden leader will help one or both parties eliminate the struggle by finding solutions based outside the basic conflict. By thoroughly understanding the conflict, the hidden leader can often find new procedures, processes, or structures that eliminate the conflict, although the emotional perspective of both parties doesn't change.

A hidden leader may also suggest to one or both parties that a mediator is a good resource to resolve the issue. While hidden leaders may not be able to help resolve all damaging conflicts, they know when to step away and when to use other skills, particularly listening, to help one or both parties transform a damaging situation into a more manageable one.

IDENTIFYING RELATIONAL LEADERS

The primary evidence of relational leadership are hidden leaders' reputations in the organization. People describe them as "helpful" or "honest" or "easy to get along with," depending on the cultural contexts. They may also be known as cooperative, concerned, and productive.

You can also identify relational leaders by observing their use of critical interpersonal skills. Evidence will clearly emerge as the leader uses the effective face-to-face communication skills we've discussed:

- **Face-to-face conversations are effective and energetic.** Watch for discussions where the leader encourages everyone to participate, through questions, requests, and encouragement to contribute.

- **Few misunderstandings escalate between the relational leader and others.** The leader, using active listening, ensures his understanding of others' points of view.

- **Conflicts are resolved unemotionally.** The relational leader effectively triangulates conflicts so that no party identifies with a point of view and everyone involved seeks a resolution to an issue, not power over another's opinion.

- **Resolved conflicts help attain the desired result.** Relational leaders see conflicts as creative moments when solutions can be improved and challenges addressed, all with the end in mind.

- **Constructive criticism helps others improve their performance.** Relational leaders help people understand that ineffective behaviors are not inherent but can be changed. They also help colleagues identify what they do well so they can continue to do those things. Because people feel their good contributions are acknowledged, they also work harder to improve performance on other fronts.

- **Thinking processes are transparent to all involved.** Relational leaders know that a unified and clear thought process helps people contribute constructively. They take the lead in explaining their thinking and help others do the same with pertinent questions and active listening.

- **Credit is given where credit is due.** Relational leaders attribute successes to the people who contributed. If that includes the leader, the fact is not hidden or covered. But all whose efforts build success are credited, both to peers and others in the organization.

Relational leaders also think about others and how they can contribute. This stems from the importance of relationships to the leader, and the willingness to broaden and deepen relationships that exist. Watch for hidden leaders with strong relational leadership who:

- **Involve those who may be shy or hesitant to contribute.** Not everyone is willing to offer an opinion or share a viewpoint. Relational leaders notice these team members and ask them for their thoughts. Either because of an existing relationship with the leader or the leader's reputation as concerned and oriented to people, more shy or reticent colleagues are willing to contribute ideas or comments. By encouraging more introverted team members, relational leaders obtain more data on which the team can base decisions. They also demonstrate that they value people's points of view.

◘ **Share relevant information broadly with those who might benefit.** Relational leaders tend to know about important events, from product-launch details to information about a new project, largely because of their broad base of relationships throughout the organization. They make efforts to share knowledge that will help people be more productive, information that helps improve performance. They also enjoy being a conduit of information from which colleagues can benefit.

◘ **Communicate to management appropriately.** Colleagues regard those who lead through relationships as helpful and open. Management may hold the same opinion. But the information these leaders share with management is appropriate to the organization's overall goals. Much of this openness is based on these leaders' relationships with people in management ranks. Relational leaders don't respond to management interrogations about others' performance or opinions. Managers know these leaders will not divulge those things inappropriately. They simply strive to connect people through information so that all may benefit.

WORKSHEET: ASSESS A RELATIONAL LEADER

Think of a potential hidden leader and respond to the statements below by circling the number that most represents that person's behaviors. The higher the score, the more likely you have spotted a hidden leader who leads through relationships. The online worksheet will calculate this for you.

bit.ly/1a2L6uR

	Observed Behavior	Frequency (1=Never, 5=Always)				
Face-to-Face Communication	Speaks clearly and well	1	2	3	4	5
	Asks questions to understand others' points of view	1	2	3	4	5
	Waits for others to complete thoughts and sentences before commenting or concluding	1	2	3	4	5
	Often asks "one more question"	1	2	3	4	5
	Shares relevant information with those who might benefit	1	2	3	4	5
	Communicates to management appropriately	1	2	3	4	5
Transparent Critical Thinking	Asks questions to help others understand	1	2	3	4	5
	Asks questions to gauge others' opinions and ideas	1	2	3	4	5
	Encourages everyone to participate in discussions, especially those who seem shy or hesitant	1	2	3	4	5
	Takes time to explain assumptions behind her conclusions	1	2	3	4	5
Crediting Others	Credits others' accomplishments to managers as well as to peers	1	2	3	4	5
	When crediting others, notes how the action helps others or the organization	1	2	3	4	5
Honest and Complete Criticism	Says what is right about an action as well as what could be changed	1	2	3	4	5
	Balances the importance of good and poor behaviors	1	2	3	4	5
	Helps others improve performance with criticism and feedback	1	2	3	4	5
Effective Conflict Resolution	Triangulates conflicts by placing them outside of the personalities of those involved	1	2	3	4	5
	Looks for middle ground in conflicts	1	2	3	4	5
	Allows few conflicts to escalate out of control	1	2	3	4	5
	Resolves conflict to achieve specific, desired results	1	2	3	4	5
	Describes those involved in conflicts as having good intentions	1	2	3	4	5
	Total Score					

IDENTIFYING RELATIONAL CULTURES

Relational cultures enable hidden leaders to thrive throughout your business. A high-functioning relational culture resembles a happy family. People within these cultures may not notice many of the relational skills at work, because the skills are endemic to the way people treat one another. And, as in happy families, drama is kept to a minimum. Of course, happy does not mean harmonious. Conflicts arise, of course, but they are creative conflicts that result from differing ideas or solutions. People are valued in relational cultures, and honest communication is easy for people within the culture, including hidden leaders.

However, as Leo Tolstoy wrote at the beginning of *Anna Karenina*, "All happy families are alike; each unhappy family is unhappy in its own way."[3] The same could be said of organizational cultures. When these cultures are relationally dysfunctional, they display specific symptoms that make relationships and communications difficult. In these cultures, hidden leaders can emerge, but it is usually in spite of the culture and not because of it.

A frank, honest assessment of your company culture is difficult from within, just as it is difficult for members of unhappy families to pinpoint what it is that makes them unhappy. Sometimes people can see symptoms. It may be a challenge to identify underlying causes based on how members of the culture relate to each other and to the whole. However, by examining symptoms of relational difficulties, you can begin to identify how functional your culture is and where dysfunctions can be corrected.

We have seen relational dysfunctions within cultures emerge in five areas: the freedom to speak (or lack of it), decision-making processes, celebrations of success, responses to failures, and the nature of conflict. In each of these areas, symptoms point to lack of relational skills on a cultural or structural level within an organization. Addressing the symptoms alone will not reduce the dysfunction. Understanding the source of the symptoms in terms of critical relational skills may point to solutions.

A strong sign of a functioning relational culture is people's feeling of being able to speak their minds without punishment. This freedom to speak is not the freedom to be mean, abusive, or destructive. It is a feeling that anywhere in the organization, people speak honestly about business issues and are not afraid of any conflicts that might result.

The freedom to speak emerges when the culture is strong in the face-to-face communication skills of relational leaders: sharing information, clarifying, confirming, and acknowledging others. Because these skills promote understanding and strengthen listening skills, they support the feeling within the culture that there are no forbidden topics of conversation in the context of the organization and its goals (there are, of course, numerous topics inappropriate to a business context).

The freedom to speak transcends positions of power in a functioning relational culture. In these cultures, speaking up is not seen as unusual or dangerous. It is another facet of the strong relationships between the leaders of the organization (hidden and otherwise) and the people within the organization. This doesn't mean that people leapfrog their direct supervisors and complain to their supervisors' managers. It does mean that people are not intimidated or afraid to talk about what is really happening within the organization when people in positions of power are present.

Dysfunctional cultures place many limitations on the freedom to speak. These limitations are not formal. Nowhere in a dysfunctional relational culture will you find a written rule that says, "Don't talk about this subject!" However, those in the culture know exactly what these forbidden topics are. You can tell that a culture's freedom to speak is constrained when there is the proverbial elephant in the room, or a topic, idea, solution, or challenge that people know is important but no one will mention.

These dysfunctional cultures generally harbor many hidden agendas and subplots that undermine communication within and among areas in the company. Business silos, short- or long-term alliances that team up against other areas of the company, and a general sense of disbelief in whatever management says are other symptoms. People tend to take issues to managers far above them in the local hierarchy instead of discussing them with their own supervisors. Secrets abound.

The worst of these cultures squelch conversations throughout the company except within small cliques whose members trust each other. These conversations stall when someone outside the group enters the room. Many such conversations happen behind closed doors or off the corporate campus.

Most cultures nurture some version of an informational grapevine, an informal system of communication that people depend on. In dysfunctional relational cultures, the grapevine is the primary source of data. It doesn't matter what management declares—the content is interpreted, discussed, and evaluated on the grapevine, not in the open. As a manager, if your culture is dysfunctional in this way, you will find yourself constantly addressing rumors, erroneous information, and fervent questions from your employees about things they've heard. Further, when you do tell people what you think is the truth, they will not believe you if the grapevine tells them conflicting information.

What you will notice in these dysfunctional cultures is that these symptoms appear at all levels of the organization. Frontline workers to the C-level executive suite will see these things because relational communication skills are weak at all levels.

It's easy to get caught up in these attempts to communicate without communicating because people who step out of line and actually discuss these issues are shunned, demoted, or sometimes fired. Many of them leave. Yet because people inherently want to know what is going on, secret communications occur where people feel safe: in small groups of people they trust.

In well-functioning relational cultures, the "what" and "why" of decisions are clear. Executives regularly communicate what new decisions are, why they were made, and how they will help the company reach its stated strategic goals. They also clarify links between major decisions and the organization's value promise to customers.

This pattern extends to all levels in relational cultures. Managers, using the model of the C-level, ensure that their employees understand how decisions were made. People determine appropriate tactical moves because they understand the strategic aspects of corporate decisions. When major decisions must be made, employees look at the whole picture before committing to a path. They look for unforeseen influences or results and strive to maintain the connection between daily tactical decisions and long-term strategic ones.

Decision making is effective in these cultures because people use transparent critical-thinking skills. They practice the habit of making the thought process that led to a decision transparent to employees. They ask questions to ensure that they understand the process. In these cultures, the decision-making process itself reflects the skill of transparent critical thinking.

In dysfunctional relational cultures, decisions do not seem well integrated with the company's overall strategic goals. Top management announces major initiatives without explaining the rationale behind them. Priorities may change quickly. Sometimes there are no priorities at all. Major initiatives will conflict in their importance, purposes, and goals. Departments or areas will make decisions that clash with each other. The overall direction of the company seems to waver, change, or go back on itself.

These are symptoms of a lack of transparent critical thinking at important levels of the organization. When thinking is transparent, people can point out discrepancies, conflicts, challenges, and situations that will affect the outcome. Without such thinking, people make decisions in functional silos or vacuums where the realities of the situations are not considered.

Cultures dysfunctional in decision making may use excellent critical-thinking skills, but the lack of transparency isolates decisions and decision makers. As this lack of transparency flows through the organization, people make decisions on small scales that conflict with the corporation's major goals. Changing priorities frustrate workers who simply want to know where they can make the biggest positive impact. In an attempt to cope with the conflicts and inconsistency, employees check and recheck their understanding of expectations, situations, and goals. They do not engage with work that might change in importance or disappear tomorrow. They tend to do what they are told more than they might if they felt autonomy based in a deeper understanding of how and why decisions were made.

The culture as a whole loses much of its innovation potential because constant change deters creative thinking. People hesitate to invest creativity in developing a solution to a problem that will be deemed unimportant tomorrow.

Functional relational cultures celebrate successes large and small. The celebrations are public, and credit individuals who did great work. Some celebrations may be localized in a department or functional area. Others may be region- or company-wide. However large or small, celebrations are seen as a chance to mark an important milestone toward a goal.

A culture that celebrates success is strong in crediting others for their contributions. The celebrations are more than just credit for contributors, though. They give others the chance to commend those who achieved the success. This in itself is a gift. It is also a motivator. For those who are being celebrated, the motivation is to do more of the same. For those who are commending others, the motivation is to do work that adds value so that person, too, can get credit. There is also a feeling of satisfaction in a functional culture when it can commend people's work in a positive way.

Public celebrations of major milestones also acknowledge an important facet of organizational growth. It is rare that one person in an organization achieves a significant result. It takes the whole organization to breed, nurture, and develop success. Celebrations emphasize this facet of achievement, whether they focus on one or several individuals.

Celebrations of success are also a chance for people to stop and take a break from the pressure of achieving. They enable reflection as well as compliments. Through celebrations, employees can identify key actions that moved the company as a whole toward its goals. These celebrations also build bridges among different areas within the organization. If one department or area contributed the most to achieving a goal, offering a chance for others to celebrate also invites them to be part of the success.

Dysfunctional relational cultures may offer formal celebrations for major goals achieved, but there is a difference in their tone and reception. When such celebrations credit one person or area too much, in spite of the support or work of others, people feel shortchanged. Some highly choreographed celebrations, like many year-end gatherings, feel stilted and foreign to those not on the podium or highlighted as contributors.

This is not to say that all celebrations must be spontaneous events. Certainly, any large company-wide celebration requires planning. The key to functional formal celebrations is how the planners view the people who will experience the celebration. Who is the celebration for? What is the company motive for staging it? True celebration is about giving credit where it is due and thanking people for their strong contributions in ways important to those people. Dysfunctional celebrations are often self-congratulatory. They become announcements similar to a young child's exclamation, "Look what I did!" They can also make credit so general that it becomes meaningless.

Many dysfunctional cultures avoid formal or informal celebrations altogether. These are not strong in crediting others at any level. Many of them are of the old-school thinking that achieving goals is part of the job and thus not worth a celebration. Others believe that a private pat on the back is sufficient from a manager to a contributor. Some may see celebrations as frivolous and a waste of company resources of time, effort, and money. (Functional cultures set reasonable limits for spending resources.) If a dysfunctional culture is not one where the freedom to speak is strong, the smallest celebration feels fake and unfelt because people wonder what the celebration is really all about.

A culture that can celebrate success effectively builds on its abilities to credit others for work well done. These cultures often impart a sense of fun in celebrations that carries over to daily work and projects. The sense of engagement that results supports the culture's functionality in terms of relationships.

No one wants to fail. In our experience, it is a rare person who undercuts his work consciously in order to create failure. But how an organization's culture responds to failures is telling evidence of its relational qualities.

Relational cultures take failures in stride and seek to learn from them. This approach is an outgrowth of a culture's ability to provide honest and complete criticism of behaviors, actions, and ideas. Because the criticism is based in honesty, the culture can identify and accept what is valuable about failure. As we have said earlier, failure provides excellent information about what doesn't work. But eliminating or ignoring related things that do work is tantamount to ignoring the failure's lessons.

A functional culture also recognizes that wherever innovation is active, failures will occur. No company creates success after success without missteps along the way. Missteps examined and learned from can prompt future innovation. By identifying the intention to innovate and the good aspects that result from an action, in addition to the failed aspects, these cultures support continuing innovation.

In dysfunctional relational cultures, failures are consciously avoided. The worst presume to avoid them at all costs. Those who fail are shunned, criticized, or fired. The organization's management takes no responsibility for the failure of one of the company's individuals. No one is willing to acknowledge what led to the failure. Did the employee get effective direction? Were expectations set clearly? Did management provide the necessary resources, whether financial, training, or otherwise? Did the person have access to those in the company who could help reach the goal? If the answer to these questions is "no," the dysfunctional culture has simply used one person as the scapegoat for the failure of an entire organization.

We believe that just as no one person creates an organizational success, no one person leads an organization to failure. If a failure is catastrophic and originates at the highest levels of the organization, we would look to dysfunctional cultural factors. Did the executive enable those around her to speak the truth? Was information shared freely? Was a team in place to support and help the executive uncover critical data that could have avoided the worst of the failure? Was the executive open to actually listening to that team's findings? These are failures not of one person but of a cultural atmosphere that disabled the relational skills that could have promoted success.

These descriptions are of the extremes of cultures that do not address failure well. In the main, most dysfunctional cultures act out against failure in smaller ways. A manager might demote someone who has failed unexpectedly. A person who tried an innovation and failed may struggle to be assigned to a project where innovation is possible.

In more dysfunctional cultures, the entire environment is one of failure avoidance. In these cultures, employees disown doing the work to avoid the label of "failure." Managers might become abusive verbally to an employee, in public or private. Productivity sinks because no one is willing to do anything out of the ordinary. Innovation certainly suffers. People put in their time on the job and save their creativity and ideas for outside the workday.

Another level of dysfunction occurs when cultures are good at identifying what was done wrong but rarely commend what was done right. This approach stultifies workers' initiative to try anything new. It solidifies procedures and processes to a fault. No one is willing to consider altering existing structures, fearing a damaging unanticipated outcome. When individuals in these cultures do maintain their creativity and innovation, they tend to try them out secretly, without telling managers or supervisors, until they are sure they will succeed. As a result, no one else can be involved who might add value and help create success.

While no company can fail continually, how cultures respond to occasional failures—especially those resulting from attempts at innovation—says more about the culture than the failure. Those functional relational cultures that have embraced honest and complete criticism on a personal level tend to respond to organizational failures with grace. They also are able to learn from them because the fact of failure is not considered an unredeemable act.

Most of us recognize that conflict, in and of itself, is not a bad thing. Conflicts about ideas, challenges, and approaches build strong relationships and develop innovative solutions. These creative conflicts are a sign that a relational culture is strong in effective conflict resolution, a key hidden leader skill.

Relational cultures see conflict as a part of growth and a company's development. Creative conflicts eschew emotional attacks, ongoing resentments, or other signs of damaging conflicts. Instead, people in these cultures are not afraid to tackle conflicts directly. By using face-to-face communication skills and triangulating the issue, people in these cultures use conflict as a means to developing improved solutions to challenging problems.

Relational cultures do not hide conflicts behind closed doors. Mostly, it's unnecessary to do so, because these creative conflicts don't become shouting matches or power struggles. Those more destructive conflicts result when a dysfunctional culture includes personal attacks in its conflict-resolution practices. Functional cultures see conflicts as opportunities for growth for all parties involved. The issue of "right" and "wrong" isn't part of the conflict. The issue of "effective solution" is at the heart of creative conflicts.

Dysfunctional relational cultures avoid conflict because it can build to a dangerous level, either for individuals or projects. People in these cultures shun public conflict and address issues privately. When conflicts do erupt, they can result in shouting matches or long-term resentments that poison future work. People begin to take sides. They feel they must be loyal to one party or another, to protect their own futures by being on the "right" side.

Conflicts that get personal and abusive are definite signs that a culture cannot manage conflict resolution effectively. These conflicts are really power struggles between people who feel they must be the strongest to win an argument. Personalized, these conflicts can be deadly to the long-term success of a project or the careers of people committed to the company. They also poison the daily experience of work.

Power struggles often entail negative emotional outbursts that damage relationships. When the outburst comes from someone higher in an organization, they can be damaging to employees' careers and efforts. When people think they will be denigrated if they don't agree with the boss, they are unlikely to voice any opinions. Instead, they will parrot higher-ups, especially in the face of making wrong decisions, rather than face the dramatic and emotional consequences of conflict.

When a culture sees conflict as damaging, people avoid it as much as possible. Suddenly, information travels through the underground grapevine network. People do not seek to innovate or explore new ideas. Changes are vetted by discussing them privately with people in power. No one wants to bear the brunt of conflict. This avoidance keeps the workplace peaceful, but at a cost of innovation and excellence.

Creative conflict isn't a personal event but a process that leads to new ideas and solutions. Functional relational cultures know this because people are skilled at effective conflict resolution. In these cultures, people feel free to raise new ideas or point out challenges because they know if a conflict arises, it will be for the good of the project, the people, and the organization.

In this section, we have discussed some symptoms of cultures dysfunctional in relational skills. Some of the pictures we have painted sound fairly bleak. They describe places where few of us want to work. However, no culture is completely functional or healthy, and few environments are completely miserable. As with individuals and relational skills, cultures display levels of ability and functionality around the use of those skills.

To speak of a company culture as if it were a behemoth usefully illustrates our points but is unrealistic in terms of categorizing an entire organization. As the saying goes, "All politics is local," and within a company culture there are microcultures in departments or areas. These are highly influenced by their leaders, hidden or positional. The skills of the employees within these areas also play a part in creating a functional or dysfunctional microculture.

The truth is that cultures fall on a scale from functional to dysfunctional in many areas. Sometimes those areas are related, and sometimes they are not. For example, you may have experienced a company where people felt free to discuss any topic, where (in our terms) the freedom to speak was strong. Yet because of a self-denying, dedicated work ethic and an expectation of excellence, few celebrations of success take place. Is this a bad place to work? That is a subjective judgment.

Company cultures are macrocosms of the psychology and personalities of the individuals who belong to them. No person is perfect. All of us have issues we cope with. Some people handle these issues well, and others suffer with them. If they lack emotional and psychological tools, individuals have trouble changing the ways they consider their lives and respond to certain situations. Those more conscious of effective tools can create real change.

The same is true of cultures. Given awareness, the leaders of a culture can take steps to provide the tools that the culture needs to change the way it works. Why would a company attempt this? If a culture makes success more difficult, it behooves its members to change it. Symptoms of difficulty include some of the things we discussed previously. Other more general symptoms include low morale, high turnover, high rates of dishonesty, excessive workplace conflict, lawsuits aimed at the organization, and a sense of someone having to be in control.

We do not claim that teaching relational skills will address all these symptoms. Some dysfunctions are based in things other than individuals' skills or lack of them. We do believe that building your culture's abilities in relational skills will minimize many of the cultural challenges that make success more difficult for your organization.

ASSESSMENT: YOUR ORGANIZATION'S CULTURE

How functional is your company's relational culture? This assessment will help you understand areas where your culture may be making success difficult. Read each of the statements and assign a value to each. The lower the score in each area, the more that area may be negatively affecting your organization's culture. The online worksheet calculates the assessment for you.

bit.ly/195kaf1

	Observed Behavior	Frequency (1=Never, 5=Always)				
Freedom to Speak (Face-to-Face Skills)	People speak freely about issues, ideas, and challenges.	1	2	3	4	5
	People feel comfortable talking about problems to those in positions of power.	1	2	3	4	5
	Whenever a problem is being discussed, all the relevant issues are identified freely.	1	2	3	4	5
	People feel comfortable exploring challenges and solutions in larger groups without vetting them beforehand with a select few.	1	2	3	4	5
	Most conversations are open to anyone who has an interest in the subject.	1	2	3	4	5
	People believe their managers over gossip or the grapevine.	1	2	3	4	5
	TOTAL					
Making Decisions (Transparent Critical Thinking)	People understand and can discuss the "what" and "why" of major decisions made by management.	1	2	3	4	5
	People link their daily tactical decisions to strategic ones made higher up in the organization.	1	2	3	4	5
	Priorities are clear, dependable, and established.	1	2	3	4	5
	People feel autonomous when it comes to making tactical decisions for themselves and their areas.	1	2	3	4	5
	TOTAL					
Celebrating Success (Crediting Others)	Our organization celebrates important successes, both company-wide and local.	1	2	3	4	5
	Celebrations give credit where credit is due: to those who contributed to the success.	1	2	3	4	5
	Organization-wide celebrations feel natural and fun.	1	2	3	4	5
	Our organization regularly celebrates success throughout the year.	1	2	3	4	5
	TOTAL					

(Continued)

	Observed Behavior	Frequency (1=Never, 5=Consistently)				
Addressing Failures (Honest And Complete Criticism)	Management uses failures as a means of learning how to succeed next time.	1	2	3	4	5
	People who fail while attempting to innovate are not punished but commended for the effort.	1	2	3	4	5
	To support success, managers give people the time, resources, and direction they need.	1	2	3	4	5
	Major failures are seen as the responsibility of many, not one person.	1	2	3	4	5
	New ideas and innovations are tested in front of many in the organization, not secretly.	1	2	3	4	5
	TOTAL					
Creative Conflict (Effective Conflict Resolution)	Conflicts are about ideas, solutions, challenges, and innovations—not personalities.	1	2	3	4	5
	People stay engaged when conflict arises.	1	2	3	4	5
	Conflicts are resolved in "public": within the groups or teams where the conflicts arise.	1	2	3	4	5
	Conversations about conflicts are calm, rational, and focused.	1	2	3	4	5
	People voice opinions because they are not afraid of conflict.	1	2	3	4	5
	TOTAL					

BUILDING ESSENTIAL RELATIONAL SKILLS
WITHIN YOUR CULTURE

Not all hidden leaders—nor all leaders—will be 100 percent competent at all essential relational skills. We have seen entire corporate cultures where one or more of these skills was lacking. Some of these companies had been very successful. But the lack of essential relational skills made them less flexible; they were often unable to deal with changes in the marketplace. For example, we have helped whole companies develop essential skills—such as crediting others, effective conflict resolution, and face-to-face communication—to help them capture larger market share after conditions made their old way of doing business untenable.

That is the good news about essential relational skills: They are observable, teachable, and coachable. For potential hidden leaders lacking in one or more of these skills, this is very good news. For those leaders' managers, it means that essential relational skills can be developed both individually and culturally.

While it is simple to identify, define, and train people in relational leadership skills, it doesn't mean the skills are easy to learn and use. The process to enable these skills in a culture is straightforward and clear, but having the cultural discipline to implement this approach—especially if it entails a cultural change—often poses a challenge.

Creating cultural support for relational skills is similar to a person sticking to a diet. Most of us know that to get in shape or lose weight we need to eat less of the food that is bad for us (such as pizza or ice cream) and eat more of the food that is good for us (fresh broccoli or grilled fish). This highlights the difference between knowing what to do and doing it. When doing it requires a change of habits, it is usually hard to do.

We believe there is a clear path to the goal, however. To develop the potential of hidden leaders' relational skills, an organization needs a clear objective. Why are relational skills important to the business? What is the vision for the ideal future state? What cultural changes do leaders want to implement? Without a clear vision of the impact on the business, any skill development quickly devolves into an exercise to keep training departments busy and check off the box that says, "Employees trained."

Knowing how you will evaluate success will help you measure your progress. In our view, business objectives with related measures of success are the foundation of any performance-improvement effort.

Determine Your Objectives

Successful initiatives focus on outcomes related to the business's overall strategy and goals. These business objectives are distinct from what people will learn, or how long training programs are going to be. Before you begin any effort to change a culture or support relational skills, clearly state these objectives in terms that make sense for the long-term life of the company. Objectives like "developing a culture of innovation," "improving time to market for new products," or "shortening the sales cycle" help you establish a clear path. These objectives link the development of new skills to necessary improvements in the organization.

Clarifying the "what" and "why" of skills to be learned and linking them to clear business objectives allows you to integrate learning into your company's culture. When people clearly understand what they are expected to do differently and the impact that is intended to have, they embrace a sense of urgency and obligation to adopt new skills.

Years ago, one of our clients struggled to be profitable. A new CEO from outside the industry was recruited to turn the company around. At issue was the organization's traditional, military-style, "Do what I say" management approach. This style had developed honestly from historical roots, but it was no longer working effectively.

The CEO determined that all management levels, from supervisors to the C-level, must personally take responsibility for the organization's success. This required the skills and courage to tell those in power when things were not going well. It was a heavy order.

To enable this change, the CEO started at the top. In essence, he declared that his last military-style order was that everyone from the supervisor level up would take part in a series of learning experiences and be responsible for making the changes to the company's communication style and culture. Then he acted on it: We developed a change initiative that included training, follow-up, coaching, organizational efficiencies, and other tools to help supervisors and managers transform the company's management style. And everyone with any management responsibility—including the C-level—participated in the program.

Because the CEO was clear about the goal, the process, and the desired result—as well as the quality of the experiences—the program worked. At one point, a brusque manager, previously known for pointing out only what people did wrong, gave a compliment to one of his employees. The person cringed, thinking the manager was preparing to hammer him for something he had done wrong. But the hammer never fell. The manager had embraced the new cultural change, surprising both his direct reports and the CEO, to whom he reported. But the manager accepted the change because he knew how important it was to the company's success.

After the CEO implemented this startling initiative, the company's profitability increased. In large part, the change initiative succeeded because everyone involved knew the desired results.

Developing relational skills within your company culture is a means to an end. While these skills are critical to support better leaders and more positive interactions, they must be a path to accomplishing critical organizational goals. Then they will mean something to the people in your company.

Establish Success Measures

With your company objectives clear, establish metrics related to both the objectives and desired relational skills that will indicate progress and success. These metrics must evaluate observable behaviors or events. They may or may not specifically mention a skill or group of skills. Recent measures we have seen include "fewer conflicts requiring executive mediation between sales and marketing" and "levels of engagement will increase by two points in our next survey."

Use your measures periodically during the time you are working toward your end goal. Just as you don't wait until the last day of the fiscal year to inspect your company's financial statements, don't wait until the week before your goal's deadline to check progress. Cultural change, like financial value, is rarely achieved quickly. There will be successes and failures along the way. Measuring often enables you to capitalize on successful steps forward and determine how to address, leverage, or diminish failures.

Whether your measures are qualitative or quantitative, ensure that they are specifically linked to what you want to achieve in your organization. (We will address measurement from the point of view of developing hidden leaders more fully in Chapter 7.) For the purposes of building essential relational skills within your culture, keep measurement simple. Focus on observable behaviors. As you define your metrics, ask yourself, "How will we know we have successfully adopted these new skills in our culture? What would it look like? What would our people do? How would it affect our company objective?" The answers can help you determine metrics that are pertinent, observable, and measurable.

Align Systems

Inevitably, whenever culture changes, systemic changes are not far behind. These will affect how your environment works. Does the performance-appraisal process or system support and reinforce the use of the new skills? How does the recognition or rewards program reinforce the importance of these new approaches? How will compensation reflect the metrics and organizational goals? What is the penalty for not using the new skills? Aligning internal systems to the company's strategic goals and the adoption of new skills is connective tissue that will help ensure a successful initiative.

When systems aren't aligned to a cultural change, people regress to old ways of doing things. Suppose an employee is training in a new skill—say, clarifying information heard in a conversation. The person may return to work ready to employ the new skill. But if the worker is not evaluated or rewarded for using the skill, and it is not clear in the person's personal objectives how this will help achieve performance goals, the likelihood of that person continuing to use that skill are slim to none. On the other hand, if, on returning to work, it is clear that this new behavior is expected, will be rewarded, and will play an important role in a year-end evaluation, the worker is likely to make this new skill second nature.

This alignment of systems to goals does not have to be complex. Some of the strongest alignments we've seen emerge when organizations establish a few processes to support the skill training and implementation. Nor do support systems have to be universal. The more they can be customized to meet each person's needs, the better the eventual alignment of system to objective.

Accept That Training Is Only the Beginning

One of our most shocking statements to many clients is that training workshops don't create change. That's because learning requires time, and most initial training classes or online experiences are, necessarily, brief.

We don't imply that the quality of the training isn't important. Excellent training experiences are important to maintain trainee interest and enthusiasm. We do mean that effective training systems simply open the door to change. To do that, clients must acknowledge the underlying need for the training, introduce the idea of change, identify what skills and behaviors will change (and how to change them), and follow up with ongoing coaching, support, and reinforcement.

Effective skill development is comprehensive. It takes thirty days to change a simple habit. For students to learn communication skills, they need a minimum of thirty days of consistent skill use before they can exhibit the new skills naturally. During those thirty days, employees need continual coaching, reinforcement, reminders, and rewards. Without those elements, systematically implemented, the training becomes an event and is unlikely to effect real change or improve abilities.

We have seen many well-meaning organizations introduce and support change systems but postpone long-term follow-up. And, naturally, often the most important part of the training—the thirty days after the classroom or online experience—is lost in the pressure to get work done. In our experience, the overall result is often a loss of the financial investment, the time commitments, and the actual change. A more important loss is the belief of employees that their development is a valuable investment of their time and energy. That loss is difficult to recoup since people will not engage when the next initiative is introduced.

We would rather see our clients train fewer people and more fundamental skills—focusing on the most important—but ensure that the system they put in place is complete, from the initial introduction of the idea to ongoing support. That is the pathway to a successful cultural change.

Coach to Embed the Change

The most effective means of changing a person's behavior is regular coaching and feedback. It works in athletics, the theater, and in business with relational skills.

When someone, preferably a manager, establishes expectations for how new skills will be used and communicates the desired results those new skills will bring, it heightens the relevance of the skills to each employee. A manager who is a good role model by using those skills helps illustrate the point. Managers and supervisors who can observe and provide appropriate feedback on skill use will hone those skills in workers. Practicing and using the new skills over time makes them second nature.

Without a coach, it is hard to improve new skills and change behaviors. In a study of salespeople at Xerox Corporation, 87 percent of the new skills learned were forgotten within a month when salespeople weren't systematically coached following training.[4] That translates into 87 cents wasted of each development dollar. Of course, those who were coached showed much smaller losses.

Without coaching and feedback as part of a follow-up plan, a company risks making a training experience a very expensive one-time event. Sadly, we have seen many companies expect tremendous change from a few days of training. When nothing materializes, they move on to the next training consultant, fad, or initiative. They waste their training investments on opening door after door and do not provide the support and learning to enable people to close those doors behind them and move forward.

CHAPTER FIVE

Create a Focus on Results

As we have established, few things make a difference in a company like hidden leaders who are focused on results. So what is it that allows a hidden leader to sustain a powerful focus on results? We maintain it is the presence of two characteristics: taking initiative and maintaining a wide perspective. However, these aspects must be combined in the right amounts in the hidden leader. An imbalance of either trait leads to a very different type of person on the job.

EVALUATING A FOCUS ON RESULTS

Figure 5-1 illustrates how the two elements of initiative and perspective combine to indicate a hidden leader—or something else.

Figure 5-1: The four roles that emerge from combinations of initiative and perspective.

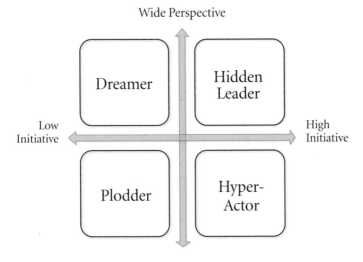

Let's look at these roles in more depth.

- **Plodder (Low Initiative, Narrow Perspective).** Each of us has seen these ineffective people at work. They equate process with productivity, and control with competence. Not only do these employees rank low in both initiative and innovation, they squelch those properties in the people around them. If they happen to be in formal leadership positions, their teams face demands for constant reports documenting progress. A frontline employee with low initiative and a narrow perspective can stop progress by insisting on sticking to the rules of the company or slowing team progress until not much is accomplished.

- **Dreamer (Wide Perspective, Low Initiative).** These employees—and sometimes leaders—are at least headed in the right direction. They know the importance of keeping the end goal in sight. But they are unlikely to take decisive action without approval from above. The result is someone who can talk the talk but rarely walks the walk. If the goal entails anything that challenges the status quo of process or work product, the dreamer is unlikely to determine effective actions that will reach the goal.

- **Hyper-Actor (Narrow Perspective, High Initiative).** These frenetic employees take initiative for action but keep no output or broader perspective in mind. They change their stated goals regularly and may profess conflicting priorities. When they are unsure of what to do, they become more frenzied and achieve less. They epitomize what the philosopher Santayana defined as fanaticism: "redoubling your effort when you have forgotten your aim."[1] As a result, they not only do not achieve their goals, they obstruct those around them who are trying to get results.

- **Hidden Leader (Wide Perspective, High Initiative).** These leaders—and they are leaders, although their titles may reflect otherwise—couple a clear line of sight toward the goal with the energy and initiative to take action, with or without approval from above. Because they let the end define the means, their actions connect to critical goals for the company and customers. Their initiative to act enables them to alter processes where necessary to address customer needs. This initiative also drives them to suggest improvements to regular procedures or approaches when they see alternatives that are more productive, engaging, and effective. This combination makes for an incredibly valuable contributor for any organization. It is what defines the hidden leader's focus on results.

WORKSHEET: WHAT KIND OF LEADER?

How do you know if a potential hidden leader has a strong focus on results? Think of a specific person, and then check the behaviors that you have observed. Add the scores for each behavior for a total score. Use the rubric that follows to determine which of the four potential roles the person fulfills. The online worksheet will calculate this for you.

bit.ly/1acfS5Q

	Observed Behavior	Total Scores
Initiative	❑ Will not take shortcuts in established procedures (-1)	**Initiative:** _____
	❑ Tends to be the person others ask to help solve problems (+2)	
	❑ Asks for approval before taking unusual actions (-2)	
	❑ Consistently wants to document progress on efforts (-1)	
	❑ Productivity doesn't match level of effort (-2)	
	❑ Likes to be in control of efforts and results (-1)	
	❑ Looks for new ways to get things done effectively (+2)	
	❑ Willing to act without formal approval (+2)	
Perspective	❑ Believes in following processes to the letter in all cases (-2)	**Perspective:** _____
	❑ Can verbalize the importance of the end goal (+1)	
	❑ Cannot consistently identify actions that will help reach the goal (-2)	
	❑ Acts in ways that help reach the end goal (+1)	
	❑ Can verbalize how actions will help attain the goal (+2)	

(Continued)

RUBRIC

Place the "initiative" score on the horizontal line, and the "perspective" score on the vertical line. Then look below to see what each quadrant means.

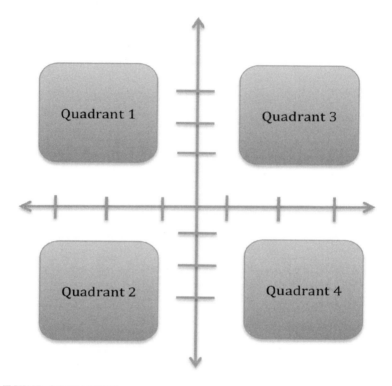

WHAT KIND OF LEADER?

- ☐ Quadrant 1: Dreamer
- ☐ Quadrant 2: Plodder
- ☐ Quadrant 3: Hidden Leader
- ☐ Quadrant 4: Hyper-Actor

BUILDING INDIVIDUAL ENGAGEMENT

When they focus on results, hidden leaders maintain a broad perspective and take independent initiative to act. As hidden leaders maintain this focus over time, they become more engaged in their jobs. That engagement spells a better and more productive work environment for everyone involved.

Engagement is an important factor in reaching business goals and results. We've all experienced engaged and disengaged teams and co-workers. When people are engaged, they have positive energy, optimistic outlooks, and higher productivity. (They also have more fun!) On the other hand, disengaged people and teams show negative attitudes and emotions, drain energy from those around them, and generally slow progress toward a goal.

Engagement happens when anyone, hidden leaders included, makes progress toward meaningful results. This progress and engagement result in people feeling happy and rewarded. The positive energy that results makes them much more likely to innovate.

The two aspects of this equation—making progress and meaningful work—deserve investigating because they are critical to the hidden leader and the organization.

An individual imbues an action with meaning. Meaningful work translates into a goal or a result that is important to the employee because that person understands the impact of the work on the organization as a whole, on the customer, or both. As Teresa Amabile and Steven Kramer discovered in their research for their book *The Progress Principle*, making progress in meaningful work is the most important element in driving engagement.[2]

By maintaining a broad perspective, hidden leaders more easily attribute meaning to everyday actions because their actions—the means—are defined by the desired results—the end. These leaders' personal initiative enables them to clearly see how their individual actions contribute to the desired goal.

Scott spent a considerable amount of time working with a credit union as it emerged from challenging times, including housing-price declines and high unemployment. Unquestionably, among the factors enabling the credit union's growth and success were employee attitudes and their commitment to serving the credit union's members. Employees were not simply processing loans or overseeing accounts. From headquarters to community financial centers, they saw their work as more significant. They helped families buy and move into homes, or provided members with independence and job opportunities through a car loan. They saw themselves as an integral part of making life better for people. In short, the credit union's employees felt their purpose through meaningful work.

As Scott worked at the credit union, it was not uncommon to hear employees talk about the satisfaction they gained from making a difference in the lives of members. Sometimes, even with teary eyes, individuals recognized the importance of what they had done for a family. Credit union members reported that they owed the organization debts of gratitude and told stories of how working with the credit union improved their lives and increased their happiness.

Such an emotional bond between customers and organizations is rarely seen in business. It is striking when we encounter it. Our sense is that in order for that bond to exist, there must be meaning beyond the transaction.

What is noteworthy about this credit union is not the work it does compared to other financial institutions. It takes deposits. It makes loans. It provides a range of financial services. But most financial institutions strive to be trusted advisers and gain "wallet share" (both good aims) without making the work meaningful for employees through a deep understanding of the impact workers have. In those institutions, the objectives fall flat. This credit union's employees clearly felt the effect they had on their members' lives, and it was important to them.

Further, credit union employees are not often compensated as much as other financial institution professionals in similar positions. They don't necessarily have lesser educations, and they are often just as skilled. By establishing the purpose attached to the work and understanding its effects, these credit union employees achieved a level of engagement and loyalty that most businesses could envy. The credit union's performance data reflect that: It continues to grow in assets and improve its net worth ratio, a key measure of credit union success.

When they maintain a focus on results, hidden leaders actually influence their own engagement because their work becomes more meaningful to them as individuals.

Because of their initiative to act, hidden leaders tend to make things happen. They see that their choices improve the world, if only in small ways. While the "big" goal may not be reached every time, hidden leaders know how their successes affect the goal over the long term. They are able to track how their actions contribute to progress toward the goal.

One clear example involves successful salespeople working in industries with long sales cycles. These often occur in selling to government entities, or providing complex, sophisticated, or enterprise-wide solutions, such as software operating systems. These salespeople, many of them hidden leaders without aspirations to management positions, regularly set up milestones to track their progress toward a sales goal. The milestones enable the salesperson to identify the most important action to do next, while giving everyone on the team—sales managers, product specialists, and customer support people—clear indications of interim successes.

With acknowledgment of progress from others, hidden leaders maintain their engagement because they get independent affirmation that progress is happening. This acknowledgment can be relatively minor—a thanks from a customer over the phone, for example—or a major commendation from a manager or supervisor for reaching an important milestone. Hidden leaders take all acknowledgment to heart because it helps them see the impact of their acts for customers and the company.

This positive feedback loop—individual initiative to act creating perceived progress, which sparks external acknowledgment of progress, which prompts more initiative—enables hidden leaders to maintain their engagement more powerfully (see Figure 5-2). Their positive, optimistic outlook infects others with the belief that they are both making a difference and creating progress toward a goal.

Figure 5-2: Meaningful work creates engagement, which supports a positive feedback loop of initiative to act, perceived progress, and acknowledged progress.

Positive Feedback Loop: Creating Engagement

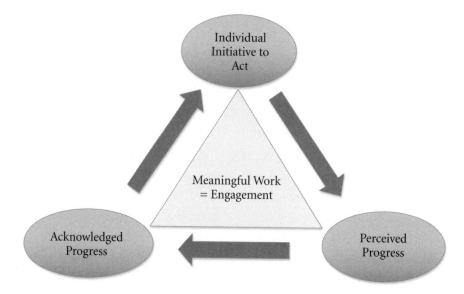

MAINTAINING INDIVIDUAL ENGAGEMENT

An engaged employee may face setbacks. Ambiguous situations, adverse conditions, and the challenges of everyday life make it difficult to maintain a strong sense of meaning and progress indefinitely.

Hidden leaders, however, often handle these challenges well and maintain engagement in spite of them. How do they do it? We have observed three characteristics that enable hidden leaders to transcend the usual roadblocks that can disengage employees on the job: positive energy, confident optimism, and resilience (see Figure 5-3).

Figure 5-3: The three characteristics that maintain individual engagement in hidden leaders.

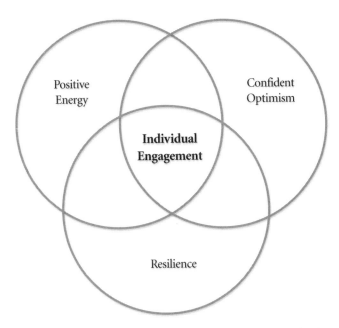

In any organization, some people simply go through the motions, while others instill passion and energy into their work. You can easily tell the difference when working with people in both groups. Hidden leaders have passion and energy, and their energy is optimistic and imbued with enthusiasm. In other words, they have positive energy.

According to forty-two independent studies conducted by the Gallup organization, 71 percent of employees are actively disengaged in corporate America.[3] As part of their disengagement, they lack energy and enthusiasm, which is reflected in their work.

Compared to the majority, hidden leaders stand out distinctively, as their vitality and positive attitudes influence nearly everything they do. They possess dynamism and drive that allow them to focus on results and maintain a positive attitude in those moments that test people's characters: stressful, influential, or dangerous situations.

This observable positive energy allows hidden leaders to sift through unclear situations and find clarity, and to deal with struggles with a liveliness that communicates a can-do attitude. Moreover, hidden leaders seem to manage their energy levels and cultivate high and positive levels when it matters most.

Optimists face criticisms of being unrealistic or Pollyannas by those who don't share their outlook. Confident optimists—those who act on their optimistic outlooks believing they will achieve their goals—sometimes face doubt from their pessimistic peers. But what part does optimism play, truly, in performance?

Look at Figure 5-4, based on data from a study of life-insurance salespeople in Martin Seligman's book *Authentic Happiness*.[4] "Optimists" and "pessimists" were identified by Seligman's theory-based test for an optimistic outlook. Both groups also took an industry-standard test of their insurance knowledge. The graph shows two years of sales results for the four groups identified by both tests:

[1] Pessimists who passed the industry test.

[2] Optimists who passed.

[3] Pessimists who failed the industry test.

[4] Optimists who failed.

Can you link each of these groups to the sales results in the figure?

Figure 5-4: Relative success of four groups of life insurance
salespeople over two years.

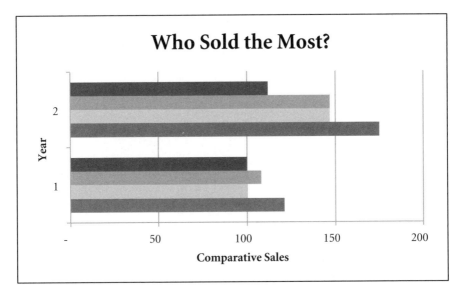

Here's a hint: Passing the industry test is not the predicting factor of sales success. (We'll give you the answers later in this chapter. Don't peek!)

Our contention is that many of the optimists in Seligman's study were hidden leaders. We also contend they had a specific kind of optimism: confident optimism.

What's the difference between an optimist and a confident optimist? Optimists can have a positive outlook but not necessarily the conviction to act on it. A confident optimist maintains a positive outlook and has the confidence to act to reach the goal. That confidence does more than help the hidden leader make progress toward meaningful results. It also influences those around her and convinces them that they, too, can act to get results.

We base this contention on our years of observing hidden leaders who emerge during custom training projects in which tens or hundreds of frontline employees participate. When we start such a project, we ask management to identify people with creativity, knowledge of the company and industry, and an ability to play as we create content for training programs and case studies. Whether the group is ten people or fifty, we see individuals stand out in the group who have confident optimism that enables them to help the group create great work, although they may not entirely understand the whole process we are putting them through. In other words, we find hidden leaders.

We have seen confident optimism succeed during creative projects. How might it affect sales? Figure 5-5 shows the graph based on Seligman's study with the groups included.

Figure 5-5: Did you correctly guess which groups sold the most?

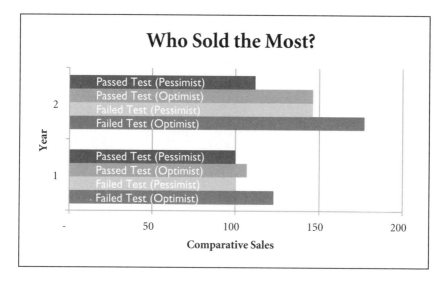

That's right: the optimists who *failed* the industry test, over time, out-sold pessimists who *passed* the test by 31 percent. We believe many of those optimists, especially the top 10 percent who outsold the top 10 percent of pessimists by 88 percent, possessed an important characteristic of hidden leaders who focus on results: They had confident optimism.

Failures and setbacks are part of everyone's life experience. Hidden leaders are no exception. But faced with a situation that might cause many people to lose heart or give up, hidden leaders bounce back with agility.

From our observations, we notice that hidden leaders rarely accept failure as a final state. Instead, they maintain a broader perspective and quickly reframe setbacks as inevitable parts of the path toward achieving desired outcomes and results.

Hidden leaders also don't ignore setbacks or failures; they respond with specific actions:

- Hidden leaders evaluate the situation and seek to understand the cause, not to assign blame. They can then address the causal factors. The same process enables them to avoid similar situations in the future.

- Hidden leaders deal with the issue at hand. While they may seek to understand causes of failure, they do not then generalize their findings into other areas of life. They do not assume that whatever caused this failure is pervasive or permanent.

- Hidden leaders seek out support from someone they trust to help them maintain perspective. This person may be a colleague, a friend unrelated to work, or a therapist. The bottom line is that a hidden leader actively seeks support in the face of failure.

- Hidden leaders faced with a failure take a break and recharge. They may take only a few minutes or several hours, but they focus on renewing their energy with an activity they enjoy so they can come back fresh to the failed situation.

Combined, these characteristics help hidden leaders maintain engagement and fulfill their focus on results, thus reaching the goals they set for themselves. The result is higher productivity for everyone.

CHAPTER SIX

Instill Customer Purpose

Customer purpose drives hidden leaders to see their work in light of the value it provides to the paying customer. It reaches beyond customer service to include the big picture facing an organization at any given point. Understanding the difference between customer purpose and customer service is your first step to building this skill in your employees. It's also critical to know the sources of customer purpose and the ways it appears in terms of behaviors and attitudes. You can enable customer purpose in your employees by ensuring that they all understand the same definition of "customer" and can link the company's value promise to their specific tasks.

CUSTOMER PURPOSE ISN'T CUSTOMER SERVICE

Executives like to believe that their organizations' employees are focused on customer service. To a large extent, that may be true. Whenever employees in these companies face customer service problems, they work to address them. To support these efforts, many forward-thinking organizations' R&D, marketing, or product-development departments research and identify specific customer needs. Then they design products or services that meet those needs and communicate the needs and solutions to those working directly with customers.

By its nature, customer service responds to customer needs. It isn't completely passive, but a customer must be identified and a need declared before service can be offered.

There is nothing detrimental or necessarily easy about delivering excellent customer service. It is a critical aspect of a company's performance. Customers are the reason that companies are in business. If a company cannot provide good customer service before, during, and after a sale, a big part of its value promise melts away.

In contrast, being customer purposed means proactively envisioning how any task affects the value provided to the customer by the company. It means being a visionary in the context of a specific job and with the company's value promise in mind, as well as stated or potential needs of customers. Customer purpose creates value. Inside the organization, it translates into customer-focused processes, products, and services. From the outside, customer purpose builds a better customer experience. It strengthens a company's business relationships with its customers, which is a distinct competitive advantage. Your competitors may be able to replicate products, services, and processes, but they cannot replicate a strong business relationship—especially if hidden leaders are the foundation of that relationship.

The best example we know of someone who was customer purposed wasn't a hidden leader but a well-known world business leader and changer. When Apple presented the iPad to journalists in 2010, company cofounder Steve Jobs famously said, "It isn't the consumers' job to know what they want."[1] Jobs understood what it meant to be customer purposed: to know his customers so well he could think for them, create for them, and capture their imaginations and loyalty to his products. Everything Jobs did was about creating an extraordinary experience for his customers. It wasn't about selling computers and electronic gizmos. It was about selling "cool."

We see hidden leaders being customer purposed throughout organizations and in many businesses and fields. (Sadly, we see fewer top executives with the same characteristic.) Customer-purposed hidden leaders see their jobs in terms of the value their company provides, not in terms of the service or product the company is best at creating and selling. That value is often a perception that is created by the customer's experience of a company.

The hidden leaders' customer-purposed approach is evident from a number of observable characteristics. Some of these are evidence of good customer service, but not all great customer service people are also customer-purposed hidden leaders. The basics of being customer purposed extend past the skills of the most dedicated customer service professional.

For example, before a recent trip to New York with friends, Laurie booked a room at the Excelsior Hotel on the West Side to accommodate them all. She had never been to the Excelsior. When she walked in with her friends, Laurie was pleased by the Old World charm of the lobby and looked forward to enjoying the "room with a view" she had booked.

During check-in, the hotel clerk said, "By the way, we've upgraded you to a suite for your stay." Laurie was surprised: As a first-time visitor, she had no relationship as a customer with the place. The suite was lovely and included the promised view, with more space for everyone. Laurie mentally resolved to use the Excelsior the next time she was in New York.

Was this standard policy, or initiative on the clerk's part? Either way, it demonstrates a customer-purposed culture. Instead of upgrading only loyal customers, this clerk took it on himself to create a loyal customer with the upgrade. It cost the hotel nothing—the suite was empty for the two nights of Laurie's stay—and it opened up a lower-priced room for potential future guests. Yes, this was a smart hotelier's business decision. It was also the power of the organization's customer-purposed policies in giving the clerk the option to make the decision, and building loyalty with a cost-free action.

Many companies strive to brand themselves so that all customers (including potential ones) experience value beginning at the level of seeing a logo. Fewer emphasize or train or reward employees on how their everyday acts on the job deliver the same value. Hidden leaders naturally understand this customer-purposed approach. From our perspective, it does more to support a successful brand than any marketing campaign.

Scott encountered this connection of brand and customer purpose when he took his daughter aquarium shopping at PetSmart. This organization's vision is "to provide Total Lifetime Care to every pet, every parent, every time." As Scott and his daughter eyed the fish tanks, a PetSmart associate stopped by. She talked with them about what they were looking for, what kind of fish they envisioned as a pet, where they would put the aquarium, and other aspects of fish ownership.

Because Scott knew next to nothing about fish, the associate could have eyed the equipment they selected and said, "Yes, buy all this and add X" to increase the sale and ensure the health of the fish. Instead, she said, "You will need these things, but not those things; get this instead."

Scott had done some homework, so he knew his aquarium water had to be tested monthly. Dutifully, he had included an expensive water-testing kit. The associate said, "You don't really need this. You're setting up a small aquarium that won't need daily checking."

"But how do I test the water?" asked Scott.

"Just bring in a sample here, every month," said the PetSmart person. "We'll test it for you."

This is more than good salesmanship or customer service. This is customer purpose, with a clear understanding of the company's value promise and vision in mind. Selling Scott the water test kit would have increased the sale but not guaranteed the fish's health, since Scott was not (yet) an experienced fish owner. Saving him that expense and offering to test the water provided better care for the fish and more opportunities to help Scott, his daughter, and the fish enjoy long and happy relationships. It was customer purpose.

THE SOURCE OF CUSTOMER PURPOSE

The source of being customer purposed is a deep understanding of the value promise of an organization. In organizations where the executive suite believes in communicating the true value promise organization-wide, hidden leaders can easily link their everyday actions to the company's purpose. In those organizations that make no effort to help employees understand the value promise, customer-purposed hidden leaders make the effort to think through what the company is truly delivering to its customers—including future ones.

It's helpful when an organization educates its employees on its value promise to customers. But when that is not the case, hidden leaders are able to be customer purposed because they engage five distinctive characteristics: enthusiasm for the work, balanced skill/communications proficiency, a sense of urgency, an owner's mindset, and being champions of change.

When you talk with someone in a business context, how long does it take you to feel that person's excitement and enthusiasm about work? Our audiences most commonly say it is about twenty to thirty seconds. That is how obvious it is that someone believes in the positive aspects of a job. This enthusiasm isn't trained into an employee; no one can create authentic enthusiasm in someone else. It is a result of an organizational environment that supports employees, provides meaning, and links work to its values.

Without enthusiasm for the work, it's difficult to build a customer's trust. A lackadaisical or negative attitude decreases the customer's confidence in a successful outcome and builds the customer's resistance to anything the person might suggest as a solution.

Hidden leaders inherently show passion, energy, excitement, and enthusiasm for their work because they believe in the good it brings to the customer. This belief is self-generated by the hidden leader, although the organization may not have clearly considered and spelled out this good or value for its employees. When hidden leaders express this belief through a high level of energy and commitment, their customers' confidence and trust increase. This eases conflicts and makes the customer more willing to explore alternatives because the customer knows that the hidden leader believes in the value of the work.

Enthusiasm born of a belief in the value to the customers drives hidden leaders to make the customers' needs their purpose. This enthusiasm influences those around them, both colleagues and customers. Colleagues infected with enthusiasm provide better experiences for customers. Customers anticipate solutions and better service, which makes them approach interactions with more positive attitudes. They are more likely to purchase and continue to buy from your company and to tell others positive things about it.

As a manager, you may think it is easy to spot this enthusiasm in an employee. The enthusiasm of hidden leaders goes far beyond a can-do attitude. Hidden leaders convey excitement about getting the work done because of the value it brings to customers. They project this excitement with positive energy and enthusiasm specific to a customer's situation, not simply in general. They consistently express confidence that the value the company provides to customers is significant and addresses important customer needs. They will also make an effort, in difficult customer situations, to stretch accepted policies and procedures in order to make the customer happy.

Enthusiasm for the work creates an energetic environment, which translates into improvements in products, processes, services, and culture. The result is increased productivity. This makes a huge difference for organizations and the bottom line in the short term.

Over longer terms, hidden leaders' enthusiasm and energy encourage their colleagues' loyalty toward and belief in their organizations. The resulting longer tenures ultimately can reduce turnover and related personnel expenses, which is a significant contribution to the bottom line. A 2012 report by the Center for American Progress claims an average of about 20 percent of annual salary is needed to replace workers. Lower-skilled workers are slightly less expensive, but for highly trained positions, such as nursing, executive, and technical jobs, the costs can add up to more than 200 percent of annual salary.[2]

Enthusiasm may seem like a lighthearted characteristic unimportant to the organization. But enthusiasm for the work, expressed by hidden leaders, is an important source of being customer purposed and an influence on a company's profitability.

For example, we were helping a company that supplied capital equipment to major semiconductor corporations. Our task was to improve productivity and reduce time-to-market for new-product initiatives. The project involved a team of near equals in terms of title and tenure from the front lines of marketing, sales, manufacturing, procurement, and design.

Initially, when it came to directing the team, internal leaders seemed in short supply. The first few meetings were unfocused, and team members tended to point to other departments as the sources of delay and challenges.

Fortunately for the project, two hidden leaders stepped up and clearly took charge of the team's efforts. They set agendas, made assignments, and promoted the importance of the team's efforts for the company as a whole. Each was passionate about doing great work, and their positive energy inspired the others to buy into the process.

One of these hidden leaders talked about her excitement for the value she felt could be created with a successful project. The second focused on the overall process, shifting the team's attention from pinpointing blame for problems to identifying causes of them and developing alternatives. These hidden leaders were obvious because of their energy and passion for improving productivity through excellence in their work.

Because of these hidden leaders' actions, the team rallied behind them. Team members discovered that similar problems were emerging consistently in all new-product development; they concluded that the company's standard process was inefficient. Together they redesigned the new-product workflow to integrate better interdepartmental communication and eliminate inefficiencies. Once implemented, the new process increased productivity and eliminated common issues that had emerged under the old system.

People need skills and abilities to do their jobs well. Without basic competence, there is little chance anyone will create value for a customer. But what are the skills that enable a hidden leader to be customer purposed?

Most jobs entail two distinct types of skills. One is the technical expertise to get the job done. The other is the ability to communicate effectively with the paying customer who benefits from the work or with the stakeholder involved in creating that benefit.

Technical expertise is usually relatively easy to evaluate because it entails a set of skills specific to the job. Accountants must manage numbers well, engineers need to know the specs of the materials with which they work, and customer service people need to know how the organization works so that customer problems can be addressed. It's obvious fairly quickly if someone does not have the technical chops or experience to do the basic work of the job.

However, just knowing how to get the job done isn't enough for a hidden leader to be customer purposed. It's also important to be able to communicate with the customer or stakeholder about the process of doing the work (see Figure 6-1). Customer-purposed hidden leaders ask great questions, not just to uncover needs but to understand the issues from a customer's point of view. They evaluate the customer's or stakeholder's level of knowledge about the problem and product or service and talk in language that makes sense and provides value. They do this without sounding like they are speaking down to customers and stakeholders, because they know that the person's understanding is more important than the leader's ability to sound smart.

Figure 6-1: Balanced technical and communication skills translate into proficiency to get the job done.

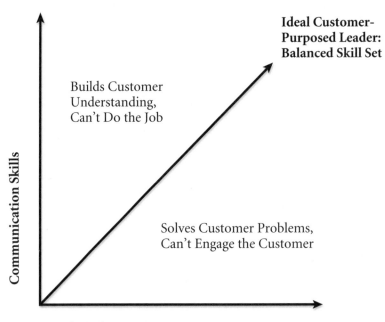

Being able to see how hidden leaders balance their skill proficiency can be daunting, especially if you are not in daily contact with them. Because hidden leaders balance their skills well, they may not ask for help constantly or need assistance from others. They do show strong technical competence at the skills required for the job; notably, when they lack the skills, they are not shy to ask for help from others. Similarly, they may have a reputation for having strong communication skills, or being able to calm distressed or upset customers and stakeholders. However, skilled communicators will ask for help when their skills are not sufficient to help a specific person. It's the frequency and quality of the requests for assistance that can help a manager identify a hidden leader's balance of skills.

Balancing technical expertise and excellent communication skills helps the hidden leader align work with customers' needs and address the pertinent issues. This fine line between the two elements can be more important than being highly capable in either technical or communication skills alone.

For example, high technical expertise without communication effectiveness enables the leader to solve the problem, but without the engagement and cooperation of the other person, who may not understand the steps required to get the job done. Without sufficient technical expertise, the leader who communicates well may be able to engage the customer or stakeholder but may be unable to solve the person's needs. Only when technical and communication skills are balanced can a hidden leader become customer purposed.

Since it is the balance of skills that creates proficiency, newly hired hidden leaders without high levels of technical and communication skills can create a positive experience for customers and stakeholders. Because these leaders' approaches are based in integrity, they know when they need help with either technical or communication aspects of a relationship. They willingly engage others in the organization to help. At the same time, they tell customers and stakeholders exactly what is happening. Confidence is built not just on technical competence, but also on knowing what the leader is doing—and knowing that the leader accepts his or her own technical limitations without damaging the outcome for the customer or stakeholder.

Customer purpose requires a sense of urgency on the part of the hidden leader. But urgency is not speed. It is a commitment to act, to not stop until the customer's needs are met. This sense of urgency—of believing that the customer's needs are too important to ignore in the short or long term—is a driving force behind the hidden leader's sense of being customer purposed.

Hidden leaders' sense of urgency enables them to help other stakeholders see the importance of acting in the customer's best interests and doing so swiftly. It provides the rationale for committing to action. Said differently, a sense of urgency provides the "why" behind the "what" of being customer purposed. When there is no immediate emergency to solve a customer's problem, the sense of urgency drives customer purpose in everyday interactions with all customers and stakeholders.

For example, the ad-intake team in a printing company was assigned to implement a new set of quality assurance steps for the ad-intake process. It meant physically printing ads from digital files and comparing them to customers' hard copies. Only then could the electronic files be sent to the compositors to insert into the final product. Team members were mostly ambivalent about the project. They saw it as additional work required for a variety of unrelated reasons, including management's proclivity for "continual improvement," and felt more comfortable with the status quo.

In contrast, one team member clearly felt a sense of urgency to get the new processes implemented. She knew that because of printer drivers in her company's system, customers' ads could look good on their equipment but not necessarily translate accurately in the printer's compositor systems. The extra step would ensure that the digitalized ads would print as customers intended. This was clearly a benefit for their customers. A hidden leader, she knew she had to show team members the link of the "what" of these new processes to the underlying "why": their impact on the customer. Otherwise, most team members would hesitate to commit to the project's success.

To share and build this sense of urgency, this employee offered to hold several meetings to review the basis for the changes and the implications of not making them. By revealing unintended consequences and highlighting unforeseen problems, she helped the team see why the new quality control steps were critical to customer satisfaction. Outside of the meetings, she talked individually with some of the team's members. She stressed the importance of their roles in the execution and completion of the project.

These actions helped the team as a whole develop a sense of urgency about integrating the new steps, which reflected a customer-purposed approach. The team became excited about adopting the process. Ad accuracy increased, fewer customer complaints resulted, and the project was a success.

A hidden leader's sense of urgency translates into very different behavior than rushing to keep up with responsibilities. Because the urgency stems from the customer's needs, hidden leaders work to maintain momentum when addressing those needs. That translates into good follow-up on customer and stakeholder requests. Beyond immediate customer contacts, the hidden leaders' sense of urgency prompts them to raise the consequences of not taking actions for the customer when working with colleagues. Finally, hidden leaders strive to keep customers and stakeholders informed about what is happening behind the scenes, especially in terms of follow-up and contact outside of normal customer service requirements.

A sense of urgency isn't primarily about avoiding problems or dodging negative issues concerning customers. Urgency is equally important to capitalize on market opportunities, address customer needs, and embrace chances to improve. Fear of loss and avoidance of pain can motivate action, but so, too, can desires for achievement, success, and innovation.

Some outside forces can create a sense of urgency. Earning business at a key client, beating a competitor to market with a new product, increasing engagement, improving service, or creating a culture of innovation are all positive organizational goals that can build a sense of urgency at a management level. That urgency is important, of course. But when hidden leaders express their own personal senses of urgency and influence others to feel the same, an organization stands a far greater likelihood of success.

Some very effective workers show up each day and tactically do their jobs, essentially trading their time for money. They handle their assigned responsibilities within the confines of minimal expectations. They are often seen as part of the backbone of an organization. They are rarely fired and are sometimes promoted. Essentially, they comply with getting the job done.

But hidden leaders bring much more to the workplace. They bring the commitment of a company owner to their jobs. Daily, they come to work ready to make a difference and help the organization and its customers achieve their goals. This customer purpose exists because hidden leaders see themselves as responsible owners of the organization, not just employees. They take ownership of their jobs and their companies' success.

When a hidden leader acts like an owner, managers will see the leader reference company strategies in the process of making decisions in the workplace. These strategies will also appear as rationale by the hidden leader for arguments made in the customers' best interests. Because customer-purposed hidden leaders take an owner's perspective, they make it a point to understand how customers use the company's products and services and, more important, why they use them. This understanding will also emerge in discussions about making strategic and tactical decisions within the company.

Additionally, a hidden leader takes responsibility for customer results and outcomes as if he or she were the owner of the company. He will often go outside the normal channels to provide for customers' needs. This understanding and responsibility emerges because customer-purposed hidden leaders ask customers questions to understand their points of view. These questions cover more than the ostensible role of the company's product or service. They go into areas that may not seem directly connected but help the hidden leader understand the context for the customer's doing business with the organization. The leader translates this context to colleagues in the course of doing business, in discussions related to customers, stakeholders, products, services, and strategies.

Acting like an owner is strategic behavior that most senior executives would love to cultivate in their employees but often cannot see how to do. Behaving like an owner is not a subtle shift. It is a transformation that hidden leaders, with their self-ownership of actions, embody daily.

We all have our airport horror stories. But a few lucky travelers experience the opposite. One of our colleagues, a sales coach, was outbound on a weekend vacation trip. On the way to her gate at the airport, she paused to hear a salesperson's pitch offering an airline credit card with travel benefits. The coach was interested in the card and decided to enroll. As the process got under way, she became engrossed in what she was observing: an experienced employee training a newcomer. She took particular interest because she was writing an article about sales reps learning from one another in the field.

With the pauses for training, the encounter took longer than expected. The sales coach, wrapped up in observing how the training was executed, missed the final call to board her flight. Realizing her mistake—and that her brief vacation was in jeopardy—the customer went to the airline's service desk. (Luckily she was flying on the same airline that offered the credit card.)

Even though missing the flight was entirely the customer's fault, upon hearing the tale of being caught up observing a training episode while enrolling in the company's card program, the airline rep booked her on the next available flight at no charge. The rep even sent her to an alternate airport that would get the customer to her destination in time to use the ticket she had bought for a play that evening.

However, this meant the customer's bag was at one airport and the customer was at another. At the arrival airport, another service rep, on hearing the tale of how a credit-card enrollment caused the traveler to become separated from her suitcase, arranged free delivery of the bag to her hotel.

What is noteworthy about this story is that the two hidden leaders focused on the customer's overall experience with the airline, not just the transactions for which they were responsible—rebooking and baggage routing, respectively. Each representative acted in a matter of minutes, taking personal responsibility for creating a stellar customer experience without escalating the issue to a supervisor. For the customer, the memorable experience of a potential vacation tragedy averted by swift action developed a tremendous loyalty to that airline.

Hidden leaders embrace their organizations' strategies—which, when successful, centralize customers naturally—as a daily operating template for how they define and do their jobs. This enables them to behave as if they owned the business. With an owner's mindset, hidden leaders see their job's importance to the company and the customer. They recognize that they make a difference. This recognition is part of the engine that drives their customer purpose.

Change is difficult, for people as well as companies. When it comes to initiating change, internal focus and complacency is common within organizations and among employees. In most cases, this complacency is deadly for the customer, who lives in a world where change frequently brings new solutions to problems.

Over the long term, complacency and fear of adjusting to the market can also be deadly for organizations. Recent business history is full of stories about overconfident or complacent companies that, modeling their future on their past success, failed completely while more viable competitors consumed their market share. Eastman Kodak comes to mind: Although Kodak invented the first digital camera, its insistence that film was its primary product resulted in the company's eventual bankruptcy while the digital camera revolution took place under its nose, building on its own ingenuity. We suspect that what contributed to Kodak's downfall was that either the culture had a dearth of hidden leaders, or senior leaders were so ensconced in their positions that hidden leaders could not make a difference.

We also know of examples where top-level management listens to hidden leaders within their organization. For example, Google is famous for implementing frontline employees' ideas about products and projects that address unseen customer needs. Google Earth, Google Maps, and AdSense—which create significant revenue for the company—were all bottom-up projects that Google senior management was wise enough to embrace.

Listening to hidden leaders can be an important weapon against organizational complacency. Because they are customer purposed, hidden leaders look for ways to keep up with customer needs and market challenges. They are often the ones advocating improvements and responses to better meet customer needs. These champions of change will challenge the status quo, no matter their positions in the existing hierarchy. They are determined to serve the customer well, even if that means working against existing systems and assumptions.

This doesn't mean that hidden leaders are rebels. They are people willing to question and press for continuous improvement and innovation because they believe in the importance of the value they provide to customers. It is worth noting that we do not identify hidden leaders as change participants, ready to comply with change. We see them as change champions. As such, they are an important driving force. They provide the impetus and create momentum for change because the customer is their primary stimulus for doing the work.

Hidden leaders become champions of change when that change is something that will benefit the customer. To understand any change initiatives, these leaders ask questions to understand how and why the change will positively affect the value the company provides to customers. Once they understand the importance of a change, they will ask questions to understand their colleagues' fears and concerns about the change. These questions will also emerge as a hidden leader initiates change ideas within the work area. Once this understanding is established, the hidden leader uses communication skills to help others understand, accept, and embrace the importance of and reasons for change and change initiatives, whether mandated by management or initiated on the front lines of the organization.

Because they are customer purposed, hidden leaders understand what is in the customers' best interests. (In our opinion, this ability has become increasingly rare for too many organizations.) Unafraid of promoting change, hidden leaders listen to customers carefully. They pay attention to the conditions that are driving customer needs. They realize that neither the customer nor the needs exist in a vacuum but are part of a bigger picture.

Hidden leaders understand the context of how customers use their products and services, and they pay attention to progress in areas seemingly unrelated to their company's concerns. This allows the leaders to uncover unseen or complex issues that could undermine the organization. Armed with this information, they conduct in-depth conversations with colleagues about the organization's approaches and how they impact the customer. They promote their insights into how the company can respond effectively.

Further, hidden leaders use their strong communication and persuasion skills to challenge the status quo collaboratively. They ask questions to understand the doubts or fears of those who oppose change. They gather information needed to justify a change and then address others' doubts and fears by asking "What if?" questions to help doubters understand the potential benefits of a change. They realize the far greater power of helping someone draw her own conclusion versus preaching to her. They encourage people to adopt new practices that better fulfill customer needs.

We disagree with the premise that people don't like the idea of change. Each of us can happily envision more desirable states involving change: lost weight, more money, or better circumstances of some kind. People often talk about the benefits incurred by progress, which inevitably requires some change.

It's not change itself to which people object; it's the path to get there that they don't like so much. It is the diet, the hard work, the new routine to adjust to, or the unfamiliar or ambiguous tasks to be taken on. That's what makes change difficult for people.

In business, employees often discuss what they would like to change in an organization or how things could be better. Gathered around the proverbial water cooler, they spend a lot of time discussing the changes they would like to see in an organization. What people in companies dislike is the process of change or, worse, a badly managed change initiative. A forced or thoughtless change process can make people rebel and undercut the change implementation.

Early in Scott's career at a consulting firm, senior management presented a great vision to transform the company. It promised a fundamental shift in the business. Instead of offering development programs to sales organizations, the firm would provide a broad array of solutions that would address everything a sales organization needed, from sales process to customer relationship management systems and everything in between.

There was great excitement and enthusiasm about this change for the business. People felt it was necessary to stay ahead of the competition. Almost everyone was interested in the new ways they would be able to support clients. So when it came to liking the idea of the change and the vision of what could be, there was no problem.

In the next year, most of that positive energy and enthusiasm faded. What had followed the change-initiative announcement was an array of misfires. New products didn't launch. Management set inconsistent objectives. The company reorganization left most employees wondering why things had changed at all. A series of initiatives, one after the other, each with conflicting objectives, made it hard to focus on serving clients and maintaining current business. Doubters emerged, some loudly. Employees worked in survival mode as the company downsized and lost market share.

Even within this chaos, not once were people upset about the idea of change to the new customer relationship management system. It was the process, the uncertainties, the conflicting initiatives, and the difficulties of making the change real that demoralized employees. Had these things been managed well, the change would have been effective and successful.

Through their skills as champions of change, hidden leaders can be management's secret weapon to help others in the organization accept, commit to, and implement change initiatives. Engaging hidden leaders in change implementation helps clarify the change process for others because the leaders focus on what is best for the customer. Ultimately, they help individuals and groups accept transitions and new situations by translating big efforts and initiatives into practical, clear tactics.

For example, we were working in a large computer-networking company. The field engineering team faced a range of problems, all related to clients demanding new tasks as projects progressed. The team's managers, responsible for controlling projects, often accepted these demands as part of the teams' charter to satisfy each customer.

Frustrated by moving deadlines and growing budgets, one supervisor began to document the problems caused when the team accepted unforeseen client changes. She illustrated the impact of failing to manage these requests effectively. Most notably, the supervisor showed that clients were unhappy because initial deadlines were missed and communication about changes was poor. In addition, the engineering company was not meeting the financial profit margins necessary to run a healthy business.

Unlike the other supervisors and managers in field engineering, this hidden leader understood that clients were satisfied when they received clear communication and on-time projects. Few clients were trying to push for free labor; they simply saw additional needs and wanted them addressed as they emerged. For clients, money wasn't the issue so much as ensuring that they had a work product that solved their problem, on time.

With this customer perspective in mind, the hidden leader worked with other managers to implement a simple change-order process. It improved communication between clients and the engineering team, ensured that deadlines were met, and created additional compensation when clients' needs required additional work past the scope of the original project.

The hidden leader's customer-purposed efforts made the company's clients much happier. Now everyone understood clear expectations for the work performed, and people met deadlines with the right solutions. The organization increased its bottom line because it was no longer reducing profits by doing work not outlined in original project plans. By being customer purposed, this hidden leader created change in the best interests of customers and the company.

WORKSHEET: ASSESS THE CUSTOMER-PURPOSED HIDDEN LEADER

Think of a specific member of your team who you suspect is a customer-purposed hidden leader. Then read the descriptions below. For each one, circle the number from 1 to 5 that reflects how often you see that person behaving in that way. The higher the ending number, the more likely you have a customer-purposed hidden leader. The online worksheet will calculate for you automatically.

bit.ly/194qQfk

	Observed Behavior	Frequency (1=Never, 5=Always)				
Shows Enthusiasm for the Work	Conveys excitement about getting work done	1	2	3	4	5
	Projects positive energy and enthusiasm	1	2	3	4	5
	Expresses confidence in the value provided to customers	1	2	3	4	5
	Goes the extra mile to deliver on client promises	1	2	3	4	5
Balances Skill Proficiency	Competent at the technical skills required for the job	1	2	3	4	5
	Communicates so customers understand and accept	1	2	3	4	5
	Asks for help when needed for technical or communication issues	1	2	3	4	5
Maintains a Sense of Urgency	Maintains momentum when addressing customer needs	1	2	3	4	5
	Highlights the consequences of not taking action in discussions	1	2	3	4	5
	Keeps customers informed about what is happening	1	2	3	4	5
Acts Like an Owner	Actively uses company strategies to guide workplace decisions	1	2	3	4	5
	Understands in depth how and why clients use products and services	1	2	3	4	5
	Takes responsibility for client outcomes	1	2	3	4	5
	Asks questions to understand the customer's point of view	1	2	3	4	5
Champions Change	Asks questions to understand a change initiative's impact on the customer	1	2	3	4	5
	Asks questions to understand colleagues' concerns about change initiatives and ideas	1	2	3	4	5
	Helps others understand and accept the importance of and reasons for change	1	2	3	4	5
	TOTAL SCORE					

CREATE CUSTOMER PURPOSE

Hidden leaders bring being customer purposed to the table, but as a manager you can ensure that customer purpose expands throughout your organization. By enabling customer purpose in employees, you support the natural tendency of hidden leaders and help others develop customer-purposed skills.

We see the process of developing customer purpose in a company as encompassing two critical steps: refining the definition of "customer" for all employees and cascading the value promise throughout the organization.

Refine the Definition of "Customer"

As Peter Drucker eloquently said, "The purpose of business is to create and keep a customer."[3] A customer (or client, depending on your industry vernacular) is someone who pays your organization for a product or service. Plain and simple, revenue from customers pays the bills for a business. Without them your company does not exist.

In the last several decades, we have found that the concept of the "internal" customer increases confusion about who the real customer is. The concept of internal customers became popular because people were treating each other poorly within organizations. Employees felt unable to work outside of their departmental silos or needed to work more effectively and collaborate on projects. "Internal customer" became code for "treat me with the same kind of respect and provide me with the same kind of responsiveness and focus as you would our paying customers."

In our experience, the notion of the "internal customer" has had a positive impact in some cases. But it has also diluted the importance of the paying customers of an organization. When internal customers drive an organization's processes and goals, there is too much time, effort, and energy (not to mention money) spent doing things to please people within the organization. While this approach has improved how some people are treated within an organization, it is a salutary and peripheral impact at best. In most cases, these efforts have no value for the customer who pays.

The intent of using "internal customers" to engage everyone in treating each other with respect is fine. Pragmatically, everyone becomes a customer of someone else in the organization.

In contrast, being customer purposed is a more dynamic and powerful attitude. Being customer purposed brings a laser-like focus on the customer who pays. It unites everyone in the organization toward reaching a common goal. It helps align priorities and sustain focus, regardless of where in the business any individual works.

Because of their integrity and relational leadership skills, hidden leaders naturally treat colleagues respectfully while pleasing paying customers. Their tendency to act like owners also means they recognize the contribution of all colleagues to fulfilling the value promise. These attributes make the concept of "internal customer" irrelevant to hidden leaders, while their being customer purposed drives them to express value to customers who pay the bills.

Cascade Your Value Promise

Cascading an organization's value promise means communicating a consistent message from the C-level, delivered in a multitude of ways, about the value the organization provides to the paying customer. This message also makes it clear how each person's responsibilities contribute to that value.

Cascading creates a clear line of sight between an individual's daily work activities and the long-term success of the company. This isn't a business strategy per se. It is a process for implementing your corporate strategy and ensuring that everyone in the organization aligns his goals and actions with the strategic goals set by management.

One hidden leader we saw at work clearly understood the value promise of his organization. He was a crew leader in a car shop of a major railroad. The job of railroad car shops is to take any of the railroad's damaged freight cars—from three-decker auto cars to coal bins to traditional boxcars—and make them work efficiently. Anything could be wrong with a car sent to the shop, from the sets of wheels on which the cars rested to sticking boxcar door slides to failing brake hydraulic systems. Each issue had its own coded defect that had to be addressed. The men and women in the shop saw it as their job to get each car out of the shop as quickly as possible without shortcutting welding quality, safety, or function.

But there were no coded defects for cars that were just ugly.

You've seen the ugly cars: tagged by gang members, dented from cranes loading truck boxes onto flatbeds, or painted in various shades of primer grey and green.

Car shop crews are proud of their skills. They like to show them off. They could have made every car look like it just rolled off a display floor for train cars.

The car shop crew leader was among the most skilled of the workers. He had been at the shop for decades, though he was only in his forties. He, too, wanted to push out cars that looked like they were brand spankin' new.

But besides his functional skills, the crew lead also had one of a hidden leader's vital skills: being customer purposed. He knew how his crews' work delivered the value promise of the railroad. The railroad's job wasn't to look pretty, but to deliver freight for customers. The longer any one car spent in the shop being gussied up, the less time it could spend making a living for the railroad moving customers' freight.

So the crew lead tirelessly taught a saying to his crews: "Ain't no defect for ugly." Which meant: Short of a safety or performance issue, ugly cars would roll out with the same ugly that they came in with.

It drove his crew nuts. They almost liked it when a tagged car came in with a functional defect that would require painting the whole thing, so they could make it pretty. But without a coded defect, they had to let them roll.

The crew lead was customer purposed. "Ugly" moves freight just as well as "pretty." And the value promise of the car shop was ultimately that of the railroad: to move its customers' freight efficiently. The railroad had ensured that the company's value promise cascaded throughout the organization, even to the floor of the car shops.

In our experience, this cascading process is something most organizations try to do but few do well. Typically, we see a value promise resonating in the executive boardroom with upper-level management. The promise gets progressively diluted the further from the executive suite it goes in the organization. This dilution stems from executives thinking that explaining the value promise once, or through one method (all too often email), means all employees will see the connections between their work and the organization's goals. It also stems from supervisors and lower-level managers not regularly helping people on the front lines link their job duties to the value promise for the paying customer.

Cascading the meaning of the value promise effectively (or, by extension, strategic goals) requires a comprehensive approach:

- **Develop communications in as many media and contexts as possible**. Common channels include newsletters, executive-message videos, and posters. In addition, team meetings, individual development conversations, problem-solving sessions, and one-on-one coaching provide excellent cascading opportunities. The resulting process improvements, stakeholder and customer meetings, and responses to the market, in alignment with an organization's strategy, can make a tremendous difference for an organization.

- **Time communications to support each other.** For example, support an executive video message with posters, innovation competitions, and team meetings centered on the message and related strategies. Follow-up messages from managers and executives reinforce the message's importance. Take care to not overwhelm people with continual messages or ones that contradict each other.

- **Ensure that the value conversation happens for employees at all levels.** Supervisors and managers can maintain open dialogues about how employee actions help paying customers. These conversations can be in the context of development discussions, problem solving, decision making, and reporting procedures. This type of conversation is common in sales organizations, where the answers are often obvious. Other functional areas can benefit from taking this customer-purposed approach and defining their value in the overall picture of the paying customer.

CHAPTER SEVEN

Measure Performance

We see the embodiment of the saying "What gets measured gets done" in many client organizations we visit. Routine measurement and reporting help focus people on achieving specific objectives and completing priority tasks. While measurement is powerful, it does have its dark side. A fundamental concern arises when management measures employee performance: Workers fear that measurement will devolve into inspection.

Often when managers and leaders are not well connected to customers or frontline issues, they default to requesting reports on any measure, be it productivity, financial values, or activity. As a result, they spend too much time reviewing or examining what has already occurred. Meanwhile, the proverbial wheels of the organization are spinning in place.

Managers desperate for metrics often measure the wrong things. Commonly, they put metrics on business performance indicators that can't be managed because they represent results. An executive would struggle to determine what to do to affect a measure of profit, revenue, or another business outcome. Instead, management must measure people's behaviors and activities that help create more profit or increase revenue.

Don't get us wrong: We are big fans of using measurement to drive performance. We have found that few things are more powerful when done well. In this chapter, we will discuss some of the critical components of effective measurement systems.

MEASUREMENT = THE NORM

Not everyone in an organization is a hidden leader. That's all right. Hidden leaders are an important source of power and competitive advantage in your organization. But there are other powerful elements, too, in the people who get the work done on many levels of your organization.

When it comes to measuring performance, how do you use the characteristics and skills we have identified as belonging to hidden leaders? Our view is that people can be measured as if they might be hidden leaders. Core characteristics and skills of hidden leaders can be helpful to anyone in your organization.

We are not recommending here that companies measure and reward employees on all of the characteristics and skills of hidden leaders. In the first place, measuring so many outcomes clogs the performance-measurement system and makes it unwieldy. Second, people improve best when they can focus on one or two things to improve in a given time frame. However, by exposing employees to the characteristics and skills of hidden leaders over time, achieving high performance in these skills becomes the norm.

Before changing your organization's performance-measurement tools, however, be sure you understand what performance measurement can—and cannot—do.

WHY MEASURE PERFORMANCE?

Measurement is the basic function that drives organizations and individuals to set and meet goals, improve individual performance, and provide a sense of progress. These are the good aspects of measuring performance and results.

There's a flip side, however, to measuring results. Each situation is complex, within business and outside of it. Measure one aspect of a situation and there are bound to be unintended consequences based on that measurement and resulting progress.

Bestselling author Neil Rackham talks about measuring performance as a way to improve, not to prove.[1] Rather than using measurement to verify a result, use it as evidence of growth or movement so you can make changes and adjustments. In our experience, that simple truth often gets lost in the zeal to quantify progress toward a goal.

Too often, an individual's goals are set almost arbitrarily, without a context that links those goals to the larger aims of the company. We have also seen people assigned so many objectives that they cannot focus on any one long enough to improve at all. Some goals were too focused on quantifying progress—such as sales quotas set without consideration for the sales cycle—and not assessing qualitative progress.

Track Progress Toward the Larger Goal

A measurement criterion must be considered against the backdrop of the situation as a whole. Effective measurement criteria emerge out of the larger goal for the situation and support that goal across functions in an organization. Otherwise the criteria may distill into small-scale measurements that return only smaller-scale successes.

For example, salespeople with quotas know intimately the issues their sales targets raise in their industries. In companies where sales cycles extend almost to a year but measurement is done monthly, sales quotas often decline into little more than fiction to maintain the appearance of progress. In other companies and arenas where cycles are shorter term, salespeople may indulge in customer pressures or incentives to reach their targets—often at the expense of their long-term customer relationship or the overall company goals of profitability and market penetration.

In clients' call centers we have commonly seen telephone customer service people measured on number of calls per hour and call times to drive efficiency. At first glance, these metrics seem a good way to monitor and track volume for staffing concerns. Unfortunately, they also encourage service providers to get off the phone quickly or transfer a call to someone else rather than do all they can to solve a customer's problem efficiently and effectively. In this case, quantitative measures hide potential qualitative challenges for customers and service people alike.

Quantitative measures can also be overwhelming in their scope. In one Fortune 500 technology organization, we saw key managers gather weekly to review over seventy-five metrics related to performance. The time spent preparing for this exercise cost the organization a huge amount of time, energy, and resources (including dollars). Meanwhile, in private, most of the managers admitted this practice was counterproductive because the metrics were irrelevant to the organization's broader goals.

Does this mean quantitative measures are harmful? They need not be. Individual goals must measure an employee's real progress toward the company's overall goal—the vision for the company. Methods to measure progress (and not end results) can help individual contributors and their managers evaluate what might help each contributor succeed. Additional skills may be needed, or coaching and support for colleagues required. Well-designed metrics can also identify other issues related to processes or systems that need to be addressed.

Performance measurement, to be effective, requires a cohesive effort to balance metrics and performance. By measuring the obvious—in the case of salespeople, weekly activity or quarterly signed deals—an organization may blind salespeople and their managers to the larger goals of the company. In the same way, telephone call center service providers striving to meet the goal of large numbers of calls ignore the critical measure of customer satisfaction with the outcome of the calls.

Good measurement criteria consider the context of the performance against the overall goals of the company. They manage, where possible, to measure qualitative achievements as well as quantitative ones. They become guidelines for the people being measured, to help them identify actions that would improve performance.

Know Performance-Measurement Effects

If measurement criteria are created in the context of the company's strategy, the department's goals, and the needs of each individual, they are more likely to be achievable and relevant. They are also less likely to create unintended consequences in people's behaviors. Effective performance measurements affect many layers of an organization.

- **Results and Integrity.** In earlier chapters, we spoke about the fundamental requirement that hidden leaders demonstrate integrity.

We might argue that effective performance-measurement systems also display integrity. These systems aim to help people, not hinder them or create useless work. They aid in driving people toward great achievements. They do not result in unintended consequences of a performance measure that does not consider the situation as a whole. (For example, we have seen employees scrambling to achieve personal bonus objectives that have little to no impact on the organization.) Effective performance measures remain true to their purpose: to help people improve performance by improving skills, knowledge, and attitudes.

◻ **Customer Experience.** Measurement criteria need to reflect the value promise of the organization. They must link directly to the value delivered to the organization's paying customers. When measurement standards are customer purposed, the entire organization becomes focused on actions and progress that will benefit customers. By "customer purposed" we don't mean that standards uniformly mention the effect of goals on customers. However, individuals should be able to clearly link, conceptually and verbally, the result of the goal to the value promise delivered to paying customers.

◻ **Processes and Procedures.** Measurements that are difficult to obtain will rarely be used as intended: to monitor progress toward a goal. Whether qualitative or quantitative, measures must be easily available as part of ongoing work activities. Create structures that capture important data easily. Show people how to find the data regularly. Provide metrics that help point to solutions. Enable employees to uncover for themselves how well they are progressing toward a goal. Making relevant data easy to collect ensures that it will be used along the way to the end goal.

◻ **People Within the Organization.** Measuring for hidden leadership characteristics and skills transforms them into the standard of excellent performance for all. It enables more individuals to develop hidden leadership abilities. Those with skill deficits welcome an opportunity to develop and become more effective. Potential hidden leaders can pinpoint what they need to be more effective in their jobs. Measuring existing leadership against many hidden leadership characteristics also helps strengthen management's roles overall.

◘ **Hidden Leaders.** For hidden leaders who are strong in many of these characteristics and skills, measuring their abilities—and rewarding them—helps these leaders thrive. Acknowledging that they are good at these skills helps reinforce their importance to the company. No matter how effective hidden leaders might be, extending and expanding their core skills can only help develop their leadership further.

EFFECTIVE PERFORMANCE-MEASUREMENT SYSTEMS

Hidden leadership characteristics are not the only context for creating an effective measurement system. But we believe they offer guidance to ensure that your organization's performance-measurement system is useful.

Focus on Results

Ensure that individuals' goals link directly to the company's strategy and tactics. If necessary, alter processes and procedures so they focus on attaining results for the customer. Make sure the end—your value promise—defines the means of getting there.

As you investigate criteria to measure results, remember that qualitative criteria, while more difficult to define and measure, can be as important as or more important than quantitative criteria. After all, your value promise isn't measured only by how much your customers pay for that value. It has to do with how the value is embodied for the customer. Create a measurement system that matches that aspect of progress.

Centralize the Customer

Create measurement criteria that are customer purposed to strengthen the link between goals and your company's value promise. Question a measurement or goal that cannot be directly linked to value for the paying customer. Reinforce and support those that clearly put the customer at the center.

Centralizing the customer in your measurement criteria orients the entire organization toward being customer purposed, whether or not individuals interact with paying customers. For example, internal IT staff (who are often as far removed from customers as possible) should be able to clearly describe how their actions affect those who serve paying customers directly.

Sometimes what seem to be simple activities have far-reaching consequences when it comes to the customer's experience. In one client organization, a hidden leader on the accounts payable team was keenly aware of the team's impact on customers. In talking to a salesperson she knew, the leader learned that one of the sales force's frustrations was that expense reporting took upwards of three hours a week. When the leader asked more about the details, she realized that salespeople were expected to gather hard-copy receipts and attach them to a paper-based form to submit to accounts payable.

The hidden leader knew that the company provided smartphones for the sales group and that a simple phone-based app could make the process entirely electronic. She also knew it would simplify work on her end, thus saving the company money. Overall, changing this process from the traditional paper-based system to an electronic app would mean more customer-facing time for salespeople and more accurate expense reporting.

The hidden leader suggested to the accounts payable team that it simplify salespeople's expense-reimbursement process with the phone app. Team members recognized that if employees who were involved with clients spent less time managing expenses, they could focus on the customer for the organization. The team worked up a proposal for the head of accounting, and the new app-based process was implemented.

Months later, the salesperson whose conversation had begun this project lauded the app, not knowing it was the hidden leader who had instituted the change. He commented, "Finally, management is thinking about ways to make us more productive so we can sell—which is what we do best!" The hidden leader's customer purpose helped everyone bring the company's value promise to life.

Hidden leaders who centralize the customer often come from among frontline personnel who interact with customers regularly. These are the employees who know firsthand what customers want and need. Because of their positions, they can make recommendations that centralize the customer.

For example, Cesar worked the night shift on the front desk at a boutique hotel owned by a major hotel brand. In recent years, he saw use of the lobby change from an entranceway where people checked in and checked out to an area where people gathered for conversations, independent work, or leisure time to sit and read. That gave him an idea for creating even more memorable guest experiences.

During a conversation with his supervisor, Elyse, he brought up his ideas. "I think our guests would like our hotel to be more than just the place they come back to when it's time for bed," Cesar began. He went on to describe his idea: building a guest experience conducive to informal interactions, centered on a reimagined lobby.

Cesar discussed his vision for the new lobby. He saw wine and food tastings for people who want to socialize, an area with discreet televisions, furniture rearranged to make conversations more comfortable, and free lobby Wi-Fi and recharging docks to draw others wanting to read or watch TV shows on their tablets. In short, he envisioned a place that invited people to sit and stay awhile.

"I like it!" Elyse replied. "I'm willing to take it to our management team. But there's one thing. Management is going to require performance measures. How would you gauge success?"

Elyse and Cesar outlined ways they would know if the lobby changes had enhanced the guest experience. They agreed that mentions in social media by guests would help them track progress toward their goal.

Social media was an excellent metric for the new initiative because it is not only a leading indicator, but derives from guests' behavior. Measuring social media centralizes the customer. It is customer purposed, strengthening the link between the ultimate goal—more satisfied guests—and the company's value promise as a boutique hotel.

Over the next several months, the lobby began to resemble a popular café. Reports from the marketing department on social media showed a solid increase in positive mentions as a result of Cesar's ideas.

The ultimate outcome from Cesar's hidden leadership was a hotel filled with guests who appreciated the customer centrality of their experiences. After the trial period's success, other managers began to model their lobbies on Cesar's ideas, making similar changes in their properties.

Communicate Clearly

Most executives know that clear communication is critical to any organization, but few manage to do it well. In our work with organizations, we have often seen posters of the organization's big-picture values, strategies, and goals line the walls. In those same companies, we have also heard employees dismiss the posters as irrelevant. Sometimes this is because what people are asked to do and what they are measured on are in complete conflict with the organization's stated values and goals. Other times, managers simply communicate conflicting values with their actions. We have seen managers berate employees verbally just ten feet away from professionally produced signs on the wall espousing the values of "respect for colleagues" and claims that "people are our greatest asset." In these cases, employees often declare visions and strategies irrelevant because the only communication they have had about them is through a sign on a wall or, worse, because their managers modeled totally contradictory behaviors.

Visions and strategies are important. Just as critical, however, is management's communication of and commitment to the what, how, and why of these high-level concepts. When it comes to communication, once is not enough. Management must continually link ongoing tactics to strategic goals and the overall vision. Regular, consistent communication at all levels must reinforce the link.

Additionally, managers' actions communicate the value of the vision and management's commitment to it. Managers and supervisors must be the avatars and exemplars of what the company expects from its employees. When the vision, value promise, and strategy are robust and communicated, employees at all levels are more likely to embrace them as their own. By helping people link their personal goals to these ideas, managers encourage employees to own their performance.

Reward Initiative, Not Just Results

Most executives and managers know the importance of acknowledging and rewarding success. In general, our client companies are eager to publicly celebrate those who contribute extraordinary results. We, too, believe in giving credit to those who are instrumental in achieving results critical to delivering the company's value promise. It reinforces the importance of achieving goals and, indirectly, of setting goals that support the company's strategy and vision.

Fewer organizations, our clients' included, are as eager to acknowledge and reward initiative for its own sake. Few look for ways to commend those who step outside of existing processes and procedures to better meet customer needs. A handful might notice these steps outside of the procedural norm and determine if a process needs revamping in general.

Rarely do companies reward initiative when it results in failure. Yet this can be the path to innovation. The so-called failure, of course, must achieve something notable for the company. It might point out a missing component of a process or product. Perhaps a hidden leader's initiative failed because other areas of the company could not step up to the challenge, or didn't feel they had the authority to do so. In essence, a failed initiative might merit acknowledgment if it qualitatively differed from the company norm in a way that could produce better results in the future, with certain changes. In our work to help organizations create cultures of innovation, we often see a common characteristic: the company's willingness to reward those who fail in an effort to try something new.

Rewarding a well-planned and well-conceived initiative is the pathway to innovation, even if the result is a failure or mediocre success. True innovations rarely work the first time. The classic story to illustrate this is that of Thomas Edison's search for a suitable filament for the electric lightbulb. According to various sources, Edison tested thousands of different elements before he succeeded in his quest. When he did succeed, his discovery enabled him to transform commercial lighting and electrical systems. Many of today's managers might characterize Edison's work as a thousand failures. Edison himself reputedly claimed he never experienced failure, because each test revealed one more useless material—which drove him to find the one that worked.

We are not suggesting universally that failure deserves reward. Some failures result because they were ill conceived or poorly planned; they provide opportunities for development, but not necessarily celebration. But true initiative—qualitative attempts to address a substantial challenge in your organization—deserves acknowledgment. When initial efforts fail, the manager's challenge is to know which of these failures represents initiative that deserves support. To that end, determining qualitative performance measures can help.

Acknowledgments and rewards must be commensurate with the effort and the results achieved in any area. New knowledge is progress, too. Edison didn't fail 999 times; he discovered 999 filaments that wouldn't work. Determining how to identify, encourage, and reward initiative that can lead to innovation is critical if managers are to maintain hidden leaders' (and others') initiative for change.

Customize Rewards

How companies formulate what they call rewards depends on the traditions and perspectives of management. For example, it's traditional in many sales organizations to reward superior salespeople with group trips, vacations, or events designed specifically for them. Remembering that different people value different reward mechanisms is important if hidden leaders are to be supported effectively.

The most effective rewards are customized ones that individual people value personally. For that, managers must interact with workers and find out what is most important to them. Some prefer a quiet commendation or a word to upper management. Some like the pomp and circumstance of formal award ceremonies in front of their peers. For others, a sincere "thank you" and a special reward—for example, a flexible day off or an acknowledgment to a small team—is most important.

For many people, thoughtful, individualized rewards cannot be given often enough. Just ask people you know if they get enough recognition for their performance in their current jobs. (We think you will be amused by the answers.) Managers must become known as people who pay attention to extra effort and are eager to reward positive behaviors (not just results) privately, publicly, and often. When workers see that they can not only contribute to the company but also receive acknowledgment that they are important to the company's success, they are more likely to take the chances necessary to achieve truly great results.

HOW WELL DO YOU MEASURE PERFORMANCE TO IMPROVE?

Performance measurement is its own science, and it is beyond the scope of this chapter to cover it here. But managers and executives must be wary of performance-measurement programs that become annual events dreaded by workers and supervisors. That is a sure sign that the measurement process is not truly doing what it is intended to do: track progress toward a goal important to the individual and the organization.

As you evaluate your performance-measurement system, remember the purpose and effects of measurement. The purpose is to track progress toward a meaningful goal that supports the company's strategy and value promise to the customer. This goal congruence ensures consistency and agreement of actions with your organizational goals.

Some of our work with senior leadership teams is helping them align organizational objectives with goals at each layer of the company. We are consistently surprised at how many companies fail to pay attention to this business imperative. To us, it is no wonder that in many companies it feels as if the left hand doesn't know what the right hand is doing. Some internal efforts go completely against others, and neither addresses the company's overall goals.

With good measurement criteria, your system will not create unintended consequences, because each measure will be considered in the context of the whole. You will also be looking to measure initiative and behaviors, not just results, when they promise to innovate a company's product, service, or processes.

ASSESSMENT: EVALUATE YOUR PERFORMANCE-MEASUREMENT SYSTEM

This assessment can help you evaluate your company's performance-measurement system. It will provide an overall picture of your system's status and identify potential directions for improvement. The higher the score, the more effective your system. The online worksheet will calculate this for you.

bit.ly/1e2aDZ3

Statements	Frequency (1=Never, 5=Always)
My personal performance-measurement goals are important to me and my organization.	1 2 3 4 5
I look forward to performance-measurement discussions and events.	1 2 3 4 5
Performance evaluations happen regularly, not just annually.	1 2 3 4 5
I clearly see the links between my goals and the company's vision, strategy, and goals.	1 2 3 4 5
In general, our performance measures are good yardsticks that do not cause unrelated challenges.	1 2 3 4 5
I regularly refer to my performance goals as a map to improving my performance on the job.	1 2 3 4 5
My performance targets help me determine the best way to get results.	1 2 3 4 5
I can meet all my performance targets without compromising what I consider to be my integrity or ethical considerations.	1 2 3 4 5
I can discuss how my performance goals help our customers.	1 2 3 4 5
Our performance measures reflect some of the important skills of hidden leaders.	1 2 3 4 5
My goals include qualitative and quantitative measurement criteria.	1 2 3 4 5
I can clearly state my organization's vision, strategy, and goals, especially in regard to the value promise to our customers.	1 2 3 4 5
I know that if I take initiative to accomplish something out of the ordinary, I will be commended even if I don't reach the goal the first time.	1 2 3 4 5
When my manager rewards me for my accomplishments, she provides something that is important to me personally.	1 2 3 4 5
TOTAL SCORE	

CHAPTER 8

Engaging Hidden Leaders

The purpose of understanding hidden leaders is to engage one of the most powerful strategic energy sources in your company. When these leaders are effectively engaged, a company creates fertile ground for existing hidden leaders and produces an environment that actively cultivates the development of many other employees as hidden leaders. A business able to engage and encourage hidden leadership has a competitive advantage that is invisible to competitors. It also helps the organization develop its productivity, innovation, and performance potential.

Developing your hidden leaders—and potential hidden leaders—enables you to build leadership capability at all levels of your business. This leadership need not evolve into official management positions to be effective. Be open for any role in your company to have the potential to provide good leadership. And when we say any role, we mean it. Remember some of our examples where frontline administrators or employees provided the impetus for implementing a corporate-wide cultural change or initiative. Not every person in your organization will be a leader, but hidden leaders throughout the company can contribute to your company's success.

Now that you understand what hidden leaders look like, you can search for them across your enterprise. We've mentioned frontline workers and their potential as hidden leaders. As you look at other areas in your business, pay attention to remote team leads, project leaders, and those who take on special assignments. If you do not have immediate contact with these players in your company, ask about them. Talk with the people who interact with them, and see if you can discover a hidden leader.

FROM HIDDEN TO OVERT

We've talked about hidden leaders in terms of their being powerhouses within your company but unacknowledged by others, including management. Once you have identified potential or actual hidden leaders, you can make their leadership more obvious throughout the organization. In the process, you will convert a hidden asset in your company into a tangible benefit that you and your organization's management can enlist to help meet strategic and tactical goals.

As you approach hidden leaders, we believe you will find three responses or types of hidden leaders in your organization: those who willingly join management ranks, those who express an interest in management and your succession plans, and those who wish to remain outside of formal leadership roles. None of these responses are bad for your company. All of these leaders can improve your organization's performance through their internal leadership, source of energy, and positive behaviors. What matters most is that your goals for a hidden leader, and that hidden leader's goals, are the same.

When a hidden leader expresses an interest in joining management ranks, begin the process of recruiting that person. Again, the first step is to ask about that leader's personal and professional long-term goals.

This question may not be easily answered in a first conversation. Some hidden leaders may have thought they were unnoticed and would not be acceptable to the company's management. Others may not have given much thought to becoming a manager and may be surprised at the prospect.

However your willing leader responds, take the time to help that person fashion a goal that is inspiring and engaging for the future. Once you have done so, you can incorporate the pathway to those goals in the person's development.

Look for short-term supervisory experiences or management positions that help the hidden leader grow more effective. What those positions are depend on the leader's present position. Some hidden leaders you will find may already be in supervisory positions but have felt stuck there by circumstance. By bringing hidden leaders to the attention of your upper management, you can help the company as a whole recognize the leaders' abilities and include them in the long-term management plans of your organization.

Because you and the hidden leader have a long-term goal, you may be instrumental in helping that leader move out of your area of supervision and into another person's. Have you then lost your hidden leader? No, of course not. You have helped a person move toward her goal, and she will remember your support and coaching. Plus you will have a space for other hidden leaders within your area who want and deserve to move up into management ranks.

Executives and managers often recognize that they need to replace themselves before they can move toward their own career goals. Yet they forget or put off decisions around succession planning. Too often, succession planning devolves into an exercise in popularity, with frontrunners behaving more like mayoral candidates than results-focused professionals. Hidden leaders are unlikely to take part. We have also seen companies plan around hidden leaders' potential without taking the time to actually develop those leaders' abilities.

As a manager, you have your own needs and long-term goals for your career within your organization. Part of helping you and your hidden leaders is incorporating your area's hidden leaders into your succession plan and helping them develop better leadership skills.

You are the best person to help hidden leaders develop the skills and abilities needed to take your job because you know the leaders and job requirements well. Meanwhile, you will be working with your manager to develop your own skills and abilities for your next position. By thinking of your hidden leaders' development in these terms, you can create smooth transitions as you and others take part in the long-term succession of managers in your company.

If you are thinking about a hidden leader in terms of your succession, it is imperative that you discuss this with the person. Ensuring that the hidden leader's goals are the same as yours is critical. Knowing that you have a likely successor to your position also helps you drive your efforts toward achieving your next goal professionally.

Of course, you may not know who will be promoted into your position as you move up in your organization. You certainly can make a case for a hidden leader to your management as you achieve your goals. Because you will have helped that hidden leader attain the skills and capabilities required for your job, the likelihood of that leader's promotion is increased.

As we've stated before, not all hidden leaders want to be in management. They may enjoy leading others within the structure of their present jobs. They may not even consider themselves leaders. Yet, by identifying, acknowledging, and commending these hidden leaders, you can engage their energy, regardless of the position they occupy, for the company's success.

Hidden leaders who enjoy their present positions often benefit from public acknowledgment and commendation of their leadership abilities. They may want a higher profile position in terms of responsibilities, as a project leader or team lead. Many people bask in public commendation of their contributions. Be prepared to provide this kind of commendation, but make sure to check with the hidden leader first. Ensure that whatever form your commendation takes, it engages that person and is not an embarrassment or uncomfortable.

There are also hidden leaders who want, more or less, to remain hidden. They do not want to be pointed out as exemplars of anything. Engaging these hidden leaders is a one-on-one proposition. These are the leaders who can work behind the scenes for you, especially with new or difficult initiatives. Because their peers trust them, they hear what people around the organization honestly think about the company and its progress. And because they have integrity, you can ask them about those opinions. They will not feel pressured to name names or point fingers, but they will be able to tell you what you need to hear on an anonymous basis.

Hidden leaders who prefer to remain hidden can provide a strategic edge for your company. They are your access point into the underground of your company's communications. They know people across the organization. They are respected and can motivate people in many different positions. Finally, the work they do is usually respected across the board. Involving them in important projects helps them remain hidden but engages their energy for the organization.

WHAT ABOUT POTENTIAL HIDDEN LEADERS?

Few hidden leaders you discover will have all of the characteristics we've described fully developed. These are your potential hidden leaders. They are the people ripe for building into formal or positional leaders in your company.

To help increase hidden leaders' abilities, help them strengthen specific characteristics and skills. For example, one manager we worked with described an employee with terrific technical skills. His scientific mindset enabled him to focus on results, almost exclusively to anything else in a situation, including relationships. While this worker was customer purposed in terms of applying his technical expertise, his ability to balance the technical with the relational hindered his standing in the department and among clients. His co-workers saw him as hesitant, standoffish, and not really interested in anything beyond his technical prowess.

However, the manager knew this employee well and realized it was the young man's inherent shyness that made co-workers see him as a bit of a snob. In fact, this potential hidden leader was very interested in how people perceived him and how the team worked together.

At our suggestion, and with the enthusiastic agreement of the employee, the manager arranged for intensive communication-skills training for this worker. The manager also committed to ongoing coaching to develop the man's relational skills. In a short time, employee and manager were meeting weekly, and the employee was trying out his new skills regularly. Within a few months, co-workers in the department began to ask this employee for help with more than technical challenges: They valued him for perspectives on policy and process decisions as well.

When we last checked with this manager, the technical expert was valued by colleagues beyond his department. His abilities as a full-fledged hidden leader built bridges throughout the company and enabled cross-functional teams to successfully address some difficult product challenges. He was also beginning to think of himself in a leadership role for the long term.

It's important to remember that hidden leaders have different goals. Not all want to be in positions of power. Once you have identified a potential hidden leader, include that person in an initial discussion of skills development. Begin by talking about the hidden leader's professional and personal goals.

Some managers think that asking about personal goals in this context is counterintuitive. How do a person's private objectives interact with professional ones? By asking about people's goals outside of the job, you accomplish two things: You learn more about what is important to that employee, which may help you link the conversation to professional opportunities and goals in your company, and you make the employee feel acknowledged and appreciated, even for that person's private dreams. Both components are important to boosting employee engagement on the job.

Just as some managers think of leaders and leadership only in terms of position, so do many undiscovered hidden leaders. They may exhibit all the important elements of a hidden leader but don't necessarily value those skills in terms of leadership positions. We saw one such employee who was reentering the workforce after a time away with her family. She had great relational skills, the result of maturity and a natural interest in people. But she saw her new position in terms of its frontline responsibilities and seemed content with it.

After a discussion with her supervisor, however, she realized that her value to the company and its customers could be enhanced if she were in a more formal leadership role. She was a little startled at first that she might be entering a new, managerial career path. But it appealed to her. Together she and her supervisor developed a plan to close some of her knowledge gaps about the company's products and processes so she could build a more coherent path toward a management position.

Some hidden leaders appreciate being acknowledged but are not eager to take on the responsibilities of management. That doesn't mean they cannot be effective hidden leaders in your organization. For example, we saw one millennial hidden leader in a conversation with his manager about goals. The worker was well educated, smart, and effective. But he clearly stated that he did not want management responsibilities, because work/life balance was important to him overall.

His manager suggested that his leadership skills did not need a new position to be useful. He described how this hidden leader could be helpful working on cross-functional teams dedicated to addressing critical challenges in the company. The idea of influencing the company and contributing to its success without the responsibilities of management appealed to the young man. He agreed he would be interested in opportunities to expand his team-leader capabilities.

Once you and your hidden leader have discussed the leader's goals, help that person develop characteristics and skills through work opportunities, training, and coaching. Make the goals part of the person's performance-measurement activities (as long as that system measures to improve skills and not to prove achievement). Look for training opportunities within and outside of the company. Development opportunities and training are available in many forms, and your hidden leader may be able to take advantage of them if given work time, space, and rewards to do so. Both of you can look for work opportunities within the company that will enable the hidden leader to acquire and test new skills. Your ongoing, personal coaching is also an important part of a potential hidden leader's development.

ENABLING HIDDEN LEADERSHIP

We have seen hidden leaders emerge in all types of organizations. We believe there are ways to structure cultures and companies so hidden leaders emerge and are engaged more easily.

Modern organizational structures first emerged during the Industrial Revolution of the nineteenth century. In the main, companies adopted a top-down, military-style management structure. A person at the head of the organization held the wisdom of how to move the company toward progress. That person communicated to the people he managed, and those managers were expected to systematically cascade the information down the ranks to the front line.

At the same time, the culture of many organizations was equally top down. Early management theory encouraged executives to create a vision and give the orders necessary for the vision to become a reality. People in the middle or on the front line executed the visionary's concept; they did not create it.

The managers in these organizations were also the companies' leaders, and in many early cases, the owners of the organization as well. They wanted and received respect and credit as *the* important leaders of their organizations.

Today, management theories, organizational structures, and the acknowledgment of company culture have changed this view of where leadership occurs within a company. While there are certainly leaders in management positions, in our view, hidden leaders are the unsung and unengaged powerhouse of a company's ability to meet the ever-moving targets of profitability, productivity, and innovation. We also believe that companies can alter their conceptual and cultural structures to enable hidden leaders to be more obvious to their management and their peers. We offer two approaches for executives who wish to use hidden leaders as a competitive advantage: flatten the organizational chart and expand the culture. The first strategy makes it easier for hidden leaders to pop up in the landscape. The second creates the conditions for hidden leaders to perform optimally.

More and more companies are experimenting with flat organizational structures. They eliminate many traditional levels of management and operate on some other organizing principle. The extreme example is Valve Corporation, a videogame company that can be described in hierarchical terms as having essentially two levels: the owners of the company and everybody else. Alternate models for this organization look more like neural networks.[1]

Other flattened organizations include temporary alliances between companies or divisions organized for specific projects. Cross-company projects, especially in multinational corporations where people from diverse social cultures combine efforts to reach goals within a common company culture, also flatten the usual hierarchy. In these projects, people come together for the short term. Their contributions are based more on their skills and talents required for the specific project and less on what positional power they might hold at the home office.

The upsurge of virtual companies and partnerships also creates flatter organizations. There are no physical signals that anyone on a virtual team is a "higher up": Participants join the team on the phone or on the web at the same level and contribute to the success of the project. These virtual partners may be short- or long-term teams. But since the visual signals of positional power are absent, hidden leaders feel more on a plane of equals and are more likely to contribute to the team's success.

Valve Corporation, for example, may be the epitome of the flattened organization. The creator of the game Half-Life, this company focuses on social entertainment online through games and other technology platforms. Formed in 1996 by Gabe Newell and Mike Harrington, the company is privately owned and has never had outside funding to help build its success.

Reading Valve's new-employee booklet is an eye-opening experience. Essentially, Valve's proposition is that it hires creative, skilled, energetic, ambitious people to fit into its culture. When new hires arrive, they are basically handed this manual and told to go do something interesting. There are no bosses, neither per se nor otherwise. People talk with each other about interesting things, do what they can to contribute to a project, and move on. The desks have wheels on them: Anyone can unplug her computer, roll over to another project, plug in, and start working. A Valve desk is like a diner version of an office: Pull up, plug in, and start cookin'.

What is interesting to us about Valve's structure is not just that it's flat. It is that the flat structure also assumes that people take responsibility for their work, whether it is a success or failure. They focus on serving the customer. Sometimes this approach works; sometimes it fails. But failures are seen as a means of moving forward to a better future. Essentially Valve is a company full of hidden leaders in many roles, and the company's success is built on its commitment to the concept that people contribute equally.

Is a completely flat organizational structure universally applicable? Probably not. Valve admits there are things its structure does not do well. But enabling flatter structures in any organization, whether formally or informally, can prompt creative thinking, new solutions to old problems, and strong hidden leaders' emergence into the light.

Flattened organizations are important because they enable hidden leaders to emerge more easily. When the company structure encourages participation, hidden leaders are there to contribute. Further, because a flattened structure makes visibility possible, hidden leaders' contributions are more easily seen by anyone in a traditional management position. While a company's business may not lend itself to a formally flat organizational structure, where hierarchies can be erased, hidden leaders are more likely to emerge.

In recent years, organizations have become more flexible, especially within short-term partnerships for specific projects. But people still tend to know who the corporation's higher-ups are. If hierarchies flatten, in most cases they will not completely eliminate structures of management and control. However hierarchical a company's organization, it can expand its culture so that the characteristics of hidden leaders become obvious more easily.

All companies develop a cohesive culture. The key question is whether they have been intentional about creating that culture. Expanding a culture means consciously developing dimensions of performance so that they support the goals of the company. Since the culture is the backdrop against which the organization operates, intentionally expanding that backdrop to include more dimensions of performance helps get things done. The more that positive elements exist in the culture, the greater the chances that hidden leaders will flourish.

With colleague Constance Dierickx, Ph.D., we have identified ten dimensions of performance that, when developed, create cultures of high performance and environments where hidden leaders thrive (see Figure 8-1):

Figure 8-1: *The ten dimensions of a company's performance capability and culture.*

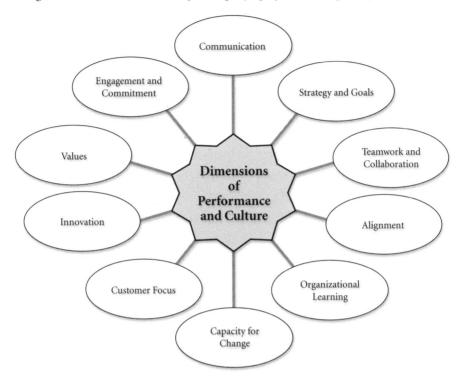

[1] **Communication.** Of all the dimensions of organizational culture, we hear most about communication. No clients have told us that their organization communicates too much or too effectively. One of the many advantages of hidden leaders is that they act out the value promise of your business and bring your strategy to life. But they can do so only in an environment where the value promise is clearly understood and colleagues share information effectively.

[2] **Strategy and Goals.** When goals and strategies are understood throughout the organization, individuals and teams are more likely to work effectively together. Common understanding of these elements also establishes a sense of accountability among employees. Strategies do not fail in the boardrooms where they are formulated (they seem perfect there). Where they fall apart is in implementation of tactical efforts to fulfill the strategy and reach the goals. Success-

ful implementations promote clear goals that cascade through the company and provide direction and focus. With clear strategy and goals, hidden leaders are freed up to focus on outcomes and results, with an understanding of what the company is trying to achieve.

[3] **Teamwork and Collaboration.** Few significant company achievements are accomplished as completely solo efforts. Success requires effective teamwork and collaboration. When functions, teams, and individuals work together across a business, they capitalize on the talents of those involved. This enables the company to focus its resources on executing the company strategy. Hidden leaders may operate alone or in groups, but they generally must depend on others to do parts of the work. An environment that encourages cooperation and collaboration, through conscious management and specific reward systems, provides hidden leaders many opportunities to use their influencing skills to the benefit of the organization.

[4] **Alignment.** Have you ever worked in an organization where there seemed to be conflicting agendas or objectives? It resembles a crew team where each individual rows at a different cadence—the boat just doesn't move as fast as it could or should. Misalignment of goals is easy to spot in a culture because people seem to constantly work at cross-purposes. Its presence detracts from the pace and success of employees. Cultures that align strategies and goals with tactics allow people to see the relationship between what they do and the contributions of others. With good alignment, power and leadership can be shared among people at many levels. Culturally, all workers feel confident that they influence the company's progress and contribute to its success.

[5] **Organizational Learning.** The concept of continuous improvement is the heart of organizational learning. This dimension of culture enables people to continuously grow more capable. Learning organizations invest in people's development so that employees improve the skills needed to effectively do their jobs. Hidden leaders look for

ways to improve so that they are able to contribute more value to the business and to grow as individuals. One of the best rewards for hidden leaders is an investment in their development.

[6] **Capacity for Change.** Change is inevitable in any organization. Embracing change as a positive is critical for healthy corporate culture. Managers and supervisors open to change reward and encourage hidden leaders who examine key processes and suggest refinements. Workers who suggest breaking established procedures are given a chance to make their thought processes transparent. To improve your culture's capacity for change, ask hidden leaders about their observations, descriptions of a problem, and expectations of how a new approach will resolve the problem or create an innovation. Question their assumptions with your own transparent critical thinking. Find ways for workers to test their hypotheses in small, controllable experiments. Document potentially positive results and open the conversation among managers to incorporate the new approach. Reward those who offer good suggestions, even when they do not work.

[7] **Customer Focus.** For hidden leaders to actively be customer purposed, that behavior must be valued by the organization and supported by the culture. When a company's culture reinforces delivering value for customers in its policies, procedures, and overall business attitudes, a hidden leader's capability to be customer purposed emerges readily. You can tell when customer focus is a strength of an organization's culture. People understand and discuss customer requirements and what they are trying to accomplish. They listen to customer needs and prioritize customer feedback. They also differentiate between the customer who pays the bills and other customers and stakeholders in the organization.

[8] **Innovation.** Management can expand a company culture by encouraging thoughtful creativity and change. While recognizing that the people who are officially in charge according to the organization's

structure guide and make final decisions, all company employees can offer critical thinking and innovative approaches to common, daily challenges. Ignoring ideas or solutions from anyone who isn't in management deflates your company's creativity, innovation, and success.

[9] **Values.** The values of any organization determine the acceptable standards that govern behavior. A clear set of values that drive the company's business instills purpose and meaning in people's work. Hidden leaders are frequently great role models of an organization's values, especially when they align with the leader's personal ethical code. In those situations, hidden leaders become the exemplars for living those values. Having values that people can identify with and translate into behaviors and actions creates a perfect atmosphere for hidden leaders' visible integrity.

[10] **Engagement and Commitment.** The levels at which people in the organization participate and commit their best work sets a culture's tone. Think about companies where you have worked. Were people willing to do extraordinary things for the business? Did they express confidence and enthusiasm about the organization's goals? When you see these characteristics, cultural engagement and commitment are high. This is particularly important to hidden leaders because they are very engaged in their work. High levels of engagement nurture hidden leaders in all corners of the organization.

An organizational culture strong in these dimensions supports the achievement of a company's goals. It also enables hidden leaders to make their maximum contributions.

For example, when hidden leaders raise unseen problems or unintended consequences of a policy or process, support them. Listen, question, and provide the means and methods to devise solutions. Ask the person to conceptually test the idea with a core of cross-functional workers. If a solution seems workable, find a way to test it on a small scale. Don't hesitate to raise the issue to management, especially when an unintended consequence arises from what seems a perfectly reasonable process or measurement. If the causal process or measurement must be altered, find ways to incorporate into the solution the hidden leader who raised the issue. Engage problem solvers at many levels for solutions that affect people across the organization.

Sometimes simply listening to people at all levels of the company changes their perceptions of how they can contribute to the company's success. Reward those who attempt to make improvements, without waiting exclusively for success. Acknowledge their contributions and provide the means to follow their next big idea to solve the problem.

When a hidden leader or other worker succeeds at solving a problem, celebrate beyond the confines of that person's area or department. As a manager, make sure the person knows if you have spoken to higher-ups about the contribution to the solution. Use the success as a means to promote the hidden leader through new assignments that help the person meet personal and professional goals. All these actions will contribute to a rich company culture that supports high performance and a climate ideal for hidden leaders.

The best organizations we have worked with are profoundly strong in just a few of these areas. No organization can or needs to be excellent at everything. While these dimensions are discrete, some build on and support one another. For instance, good alignment allows for collaboration and teamwork. High levels of engagement reinforce customer focus. To foster an expanded culture, ensure that few of these areas of focus are severely lacking. A complete absence of one or more of these dimensions can have negative implications for a business. On the other hand, expanding a culture through these dimensions helps raise people's awareness of their contributions and sparks creativity throughout the organization.

Epilogue

Making the Hidden Visible

The Hidden Leader posits two important ideas. First, unacknowledged leaders are energy and innovation powerhouses in organizations; someone's contribution to the value of a business need not be constrained by that person's position on the organizational chart. Second, wise management can maximize the power of hidden leaders to create a more successful company.

By making hidden leaders visible, a manager influences the company's overall culture. Although formal hierarchies remain in place, hidden leaders' impact extends beyond their formal positions. When hidden leaders are overt, the organization integrates their collective power throughout the organization.

Hidden leaders are an existing internal asset that requires little additional investment for payback. By cultivating and supporting hidden leaders and developing their talents strategically, you can leverage them for the betterment of the business. They are a unique and powerful source of competitive advantage.

We do not believe that hidden leaders made visible are some kind of silver bullet, an answer to everything plaguing a company. Innovation and success depend on more than leaders. Technological ability, distribution networks, a strong value promise, efficient and effective processes, management vision and integrity, and fortuitous timing in the marketplace each influence an organization's success. But because companies comprise people working in concert (we hope!), hidden leaders made visible can contribute much, along with these other elements.

Whether alert management can see and tap into the hidden leaders across an organization depends on its insight, culture, and initiative. Ironically, to capitalize on hidden leaders as a competitive advantage, an organization must have good leadership in formal positions. These leaders' vision must transcend a company's top-down formalism and embrace the powers of its hidden leadership.

By virtue of their relational leadership, hidden leaders become nodes in a complex network of relationships. Acknowledging their presence defines a role threaded between frontline employees and positional management that, however informal, powers both. It affects how ideas and innovations flow. It influences solutions to challenges. It also empowers hidden leaders to speak out for both sides, potentially connecting the two. A strong corps of hidden leaders, made visible, may become the eyes and ears of employees and managers. They may smooth communications and help deter falsehoods and rumors that damage ongoing success. They may also alert management to potential market opportunities and hazards that, handled quickly, can promote success.

This middle field that hidden leaders occupy may also push management into being more responsible for itself. By giving voice to the front lines, hidden leaders raise issues that managers must address. Critical conflicts, discrepancies, discontent, and low morale may become obvious. Knowing that management knows, some employees may press for cultural changes and better working environments. If, as we suggest, hidden leaders engage unharnessed power, management must be aware that the power may not extend in the direction that managers want. An executive uncomfortable with this power or direction could benefit from serious introspection to understand what drives both the direction of change and the manager's resistance to it.

Developing hidden leaders alters the flow of leadership in an organization. As we have discussed, traditional leadership was acknowledged from the top down in a business. With active hidden leaders, leadership circulates from a variety of sources, with influence and impact coming from directions unrelated to positions. Channeled effectively, this leadership enables an organization to step ahead of its competition. Suppressed or ignored, the leadership is likely to fade away through attrition, to the detriment of the company left behind.

We hear frequently from companies that they value their people. Too often, that is merely a platitude. Cultivating leadership throughout your business by identifying and developing hidden leaders transforms that platitude into a reality.

Could hidden leaders made visible become dangerous to the organization as a whole? We doubt it. They may challenge stagnant processes, absence of customer focus, diffidence, and unethical cultural behaviors. None of these can exist in an innovative company. By revealing and developing hidden leaders, a company is more likely to transform itself and innovate within its market.

On the other hand, hidden leaders can point out dysfunctional behaviors or microcultures. They may make manipulative, insecure, or abusive managers feel threatened. When hidden leaders prompt managers to make cultural and organizational changes, they threaten the power status quo. Inflexible or ineffective managers in these situations may offer to jettison the hidden leaders in spite of the competitive advantage the leaders might bring to an organization. They may be hypercritical of hidden leaders as a means of protecting their turf. A wise executive pays attention to how often any one manager or positional leader defames potential hidden leaders. Instead of firing the hidden leader, it might be time for skill and professional development for the positional one.

A culture of innovation creates change in many areas. Appeal to hidden leaders and be prepared for new ways of looking at the company's business. Woe to the company whose managers are frightened by this prospect. By not accepting change, an organization dooms itself to repeating the past while the world and its markets surge by.

What is more likely is that unleashed hidden leaders will significantly improve your business. They can help you leverage your company's strengths and create an environment in which employees' contributions surge past the minimum requirements of their jobs. Active and acknowledged hidden leaders can also boost morale by virtue of their relationships, their energy, and the reality that management is able to hear what employees have to say, for better or for worse.

Whether or not a manager takes this book to heart, hidden leaders exist. They are at work in your organization now. Based on their demonstrated integrity, they are questioning conclusions and driving issues to the fore. They are harnessing people's energy and power to get good work done, using relational skills, a focus on results, and customer purpose. They make the work experience better for those in contact with them. They may or may not meld with your company's culture perfectly, but they are there. Ignoring their influence may help maintain the status quo. It will also limit the value of your organization. By discovering and developing hidden leaders, and acknowledging their contributions, you can expand both culture and value to fulfill your company's potential.

Acknowledgments

SCOTT EDINGER

This book began during a conversation I had with a colleague from my Coopers & Lybrand (now PricewaterhouseCoopers) days. Bob Eichenberg, now a director in the PricewaterhouseCoopers Atlanta office, described a project he was implementing in the area of reverse mentoring. How interesting, I thought: leadership coming from associates in the firm rather than from partners. Typically when one notices something for the first time, one begins to see it everywhere. I started to see leadership sprouting up in client organizations and companies.

Deciding to write an article about the topic, I contacted my editor at *Harvard Business Review,* Andrea Ovans, who helped me shape the idea for my *Review* blog post, *Find the Reverse Leaders in Your Midst.* I'll take the opportunity here to thank her for her continued support and for helping me become a better writer. Her critiques and feedback never fail to stretch my thinking and further develop my ideas.

Simultaneously, I was working on a project with Laurie Sain, who pointed out that this could be a great idea for a book. I was doubtful. I've long believed that too many books are articles that got carried away unnecessarily. I wasn't sure it could be done. Laurie then shared with me some ideas for a draft table of contents, and we were on our way. Working with Laurie on this book has been an absolute pleasure. If we have been successful in creating a book together that has one voice, it is to her credit.

Of course, this book had to find a home. Special thanks go to our agent, John Willig, for helping us refine our ideas and find that home with AMACOM. I'd also like to thank Christina Parisi and Stephen Power of AMACOM, who recognized the potential for *The Hidden Leader* and helped us see it through to fruition.

My sincere gratitude to the clients of Edinger Consulting Group for allowing me to see your hidden leaders in action and providing me with rich examples of their impact. Without them this book would simply be another impractical theory.

I've had many colleagues who influenced me, but they are too numerous to call out by name. You know who you are.

Finally, my deepest appreciation goes to Christy, for her love, support, companionship, and humor. Without her, none of my work would be possible.

LAURIE SAIN

In a sense, *The Hidden Leader* culminates my experiences from many years working as a consultant in the corporate world. Thanking everyone who helped me live through those experiences is impossible, but I want to acknowledge their influence on my thinking and ideas, clients and colleagues alike.

Special thanks to two colleagues who reviewed the manuscript and gave valuable feedback about its content and structure: Julia Sweeney and Joe Trueblood. In spite of your busy consulting work and lives, you managed to read the work and help it come to life.

Those who helped me build a sense of marketing the book include Paula McCormick of McCormick Marketing and Julie Cornia of Black Dog Marketing. Special thanks to Erik Hansen for support and an understanding of the business, Nevin Berger for his help in early concepts of the online experience, and William Hastings of Fremont Information Systems, who constructed the preliminary website.

I am indebted to Tom Peters for supporting this latest project of mine. An important set of thanks goes to others who supported the book in its early stages, including Shelley Dolley, Jeff Snipes, and Scott Blanchard. I can't thank our literary agent, John Willig, enough for taking us on and showing me, especially, the ropes. AMACOM editors Christina Parisi and Stephen Power skillfully guided me through the process and answered my many questions with equanimity.

Many people have been involved in educating me about hidden leaders during the course of my decades-long career. Hundreds of engagements with people in all kinds of companies helped me identify the importance and characteristics of hidden leadership. Some were managers, many were hidden leaders themselves, and all were instrumental in helping me understand how people interact in a corporate environment. This includes my work with memorable client companies over the years: AchieveGlobal (once Learning International), the Union Pacific and other railroad companies, Fidelity Investments, Charles Schwab, American Presidents Line, Apple, Ethel M Chocolates, Octel Communications, Weyerhauser, and many others, some of which are mentioned in the pages of this book.

Sadly, my 2008 office fire (thank you again, Leslie Calkins of State Farm, for helping me recover!) destroyed my contact information for most of the people I've known who were fun to work with, great learning experiences, and supporters for many years. If I've missed you specifically, I must blame the omission on that. I remember you and our work together, however, and they are some of my most cherished professional memories.

I can name a few of the people who helped me develop as a consultant, educator, and, hopefully, leader, including Carol Burke, Steve Lunz, Christopher Lydon, Susan McGowan, Scott Munson, Ed Odachowski ("Mr. Food"), Linda Osborne, Paul Ryder, and Colleen VanDyke. Others who were incomparable in their generosity to teach include Chris Aadnesen, Jason Briggs, Jim Bruno, Bruce Bunderson, Dominic Coletto, Evans Cottman, Kathy David, Ed Del Gato, John Fishback, Joe Folkman, Gina Budde Gardner, Lisa Gatti, Alison Greenhouse, Everett Harper, Kurt Hine, Lisa Hoopes, Judi Hornett, Jim Kenefick, Mary Ann Kipp, Rob Martyn, Mary Ann Masarech, Jim McCormick, Rich Meyers, Jerry Pujals, Chuck Quakenbush, Chris Rice, John Rovens, Carol Rush, Carla Snyder, Thiagi, Janet Williams, Diane Wolverton, Joe Wozniak, and Jack Zenger.

Additional experiences adapting the work of great authors to an online format expanded my sense of leadership and management. It was an honor to work with the early gurus of Ninth House Network, including Tom Peters, Ken Blanchard, Peter Senge, Jon Katzenbach, Larraine Segil, Joseph Rosse, Robert Levin, and Clifton Taulbert.

This book could not have been born without my coauthor, Scott. Working virtually was never a challenge. Thanks for accepting my electronic red pen so gracefully. Our individual ideas interacted and recombined to create a work that is more than the sum of its initial parts.

Finally, but as important as anyone, thank you to my devoted friends and family who energetically enthused about this project and managed to keep me fed and sane (pardon the expression) throughout the book's development: husband Craig Bromley; the incomparable Club Cul members Perry and Richard Cook, Bill and Catharon Oviatt, Forrest and Gina Mark, Paula McCormick, and Dennis Vandenbos; and friends Christy Stillwell and Tim Tripp, Debbie East, Leslie Van Barselaar, and Deb Phenecie. Thanks, too, to manager Caitlyn Heryford and owner Jim Mitchell at Lander's Cowfish restaurant for their flexibility in providing me time off from my adult beverage engineer duties to get some writing done.

Appendix

Tools to Discover and Develop Hidden Leaders

Throughout this book, you have seen and perhaps used the worksheets and assessments embedded in various chapters to evaluate a specific hidden leader, yourself, or your organization's culture. Hopefully, these tools provided you some insights into the concepts of *The Hidden Leader* and deepened your understanding of how you can discover and develop hidden leaders for the benefit of your organization, yourself, and the hidden leaders.

This appendix organizes all of the tools into a succinct process that will further help you discover and develop hidden leaders in your organization. The process entails three steps:

[1] Discover specific individuals who have the highest potential to be or become hidden leaders.

[2] Evaluate specific hidden leaders to determine and support their strengths and identify potential areas for improvement in order to develop them into full-fledged hidden leaders.

[3] Determine how well your company culture supports hidden leaders, and identify ways you can improve specific cultural aspects or processes to help hidden leadership thrive overall.

The tools in this appendix are organized around this process. The following chart leads you through the process and identifies which tool to use, when, and how. If you have already completed some portions of the process, review the "When you want to . . ." column to see what each tool will accomplish. Note the "How to use" column for insights into the best ways to apply each tool, and what you can do with the results.

THE PROCESS

Discover the Hidden Leader		
Use this tool...	*When you want to...*	*How to use*
Identify Integrity (page 197)	... discover a hidden leader.	Keep an open mind. Respond quickly. Focus on a group of people, an area, or department.
What Kind of Leader? (pages 198-199)	... evaluate a specific person for a focus on results in terms of initiative and perspective.	Review observed behaviors on the tool. Note a specific person's actions over 7-10 days. Score and use rubric to determine what kind of leader the person is.
Assess a Relational Leader (page 200)	... evaluate a specific person for relational leadership skills.	Review observed behaviors on the tool. Note a specific person's actions over 7-10 days. Score.
Assess the Customer-Purposed Hidden Leader (page 201)	... evaluate a specific person for the basics of being customer purposed.	Review observed behaviors on the tool. Note a specific person's actions over 7-10 days. Score.

Develop the Hidden Leader		
Use this tool...	*When you want to...*	*How to use*
Evaluate A Hidden Leader (pages 202-205)	... assess an identified hidden leader to determine strengths and goals for improvement	Give copies of the tool to the hidden leader and a trusted colleague. Review the tool. Note the hidden leader's actions over 7-10 days. Score. Ask the hidden leader and colleague for their scores. Compare, contrast, and conclude. *Note:* Simplify and focus by using specific portions of the tool.

Support the Hidden Leader		
Use this tool...	*When you want to...*	*How to use*
Evaluate Your Company's Integrity (page 206)	...evaluate your culture's integrity and how it supports hidden leaders.	Respond thoughtfully, identifying specific events to support your ratings. Research if necessary. Score. Use as a basis for management discussion.
Your Organization's Culture (pages 207-208)	...discover how well your company supports relational leaders.	Review observed behaviors on the tool. Note when they occur over 7-10 days. Score. Use as a basis for management discussion. *Note:* Simplify and focus by using specific portions of the tool.
Evaluate Your Performance-Measurement System (page 209)	...assess your company's performance-measurement system's effectiveness for developing all employees.	Respond thoughtfully, identifying specific events to support your ratings. Research if necessary. Score. Use as a basis for management discussion.

WORKSHEET: IDENTIFY INTEGRITY

Use the worksheet below to help identify potential hidden leaders who demonstrate integrity in your organization. Answer each question without too much thought. You will remember the hidden leaders you've unknowingly interacted with or heard about. The online worksheet enables you to print or share your results.

bit.ly/GFJUpm

Answer this question...	By identifying a specific person
(Answer by identifying the first person who comes to mind.)	(Write a function or job title if you wish to protect the person's identity.)
A work team is stuck with a process problem. Who would its members ask outside of the team for help?	
A project faces a potential conflict of interest. Who raised the issue in the first place to the project team?	
When your team must make a decision without all the facts, to whom do the members go for advice?	
Who in your work group will dependably make decisions or act to address a problem?	
Who in your work group would you ask to identify someone who might be good for a specific role or project?	
Who in your organization is known for honesty? Collaboration? Ingenuity?	
If you wanted to understand what someone in another function does, who might you ask in your company?	
Who did you name most often?	

WORKSHEET: WHAT KIND OF LEADER?

How do you know if a potential hidden leader has a strong focus on results? Think of a specific person, and then check the behaviors that you have observed. Add the scores for each behavior for a total score. Use the rubric that follows to determine which of the four potential roles the person fulfills. The online worksheet will calculate this for you.

bit.ly/1acfS5Q

	Observed Behavior	Total Scores
Initiative	❑ Will not take shortcuts in established procedures (-1)	Initiative:
	❑ Tends to be the person others ask to help solve problems (+2)	
	❑ Asks for approval before taking unusual actions (-2)	
	❑ Consistently wants to document progress on efforts (-1)	
	❑ Productivity doesn't match level of effort (-2)	_____
	❑ Likes to be in control of efforts and results (-1)	
	❑ Looks for new ways to get things done effectively (+2)	
	❑ Willing to act without formal approval (+2)	
Perspective	❑ Believes in following processes to the letter in all cases (-2)	Perspective:
	❑ Can verbalize the importance of the end goal (+1)	
	❑ Cannot consistently identify actions that will help reach the goal (-2)	
	❑ Acts in ways that help reach the end goal (+1)	_____
	❑ Can verbalize how actions will help attain the goal (+2)	

(Continued)

RUBRIC

Place the "initiative" score on the horizontal line, and the "perspective" score on the vertical line. Then look below to see what each quadrant means.

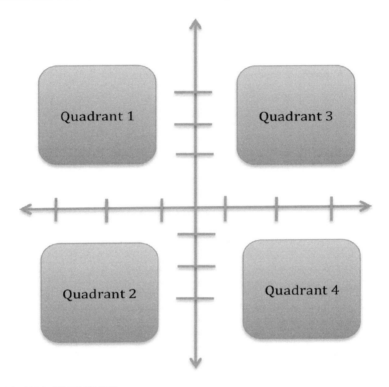

WHAT KIND OF LEADER?

- ☐ Quadrant 1: Dreamer
- ☐ Quadrant 2: Plodder
- ☐ Quadrant 3: Hidden Leader
- ☐ Quadrant 4: Hyper-Actor

WORKSHEET: ASSESS A RELATIONAL LEADER

Think of a potential hidden leader and respond to the statements below by circling the number that most represents that person's behaviors. The higher the score, the more likely you have spotted a hidden leader who leads through relationships. The online worksheet will calculate this for you.

bit.ly/1a2L6uR

	Observed Behavior	Frequency (1=Never, 5=Always)				
Face-to-Face Communication	Speaks clearly and well	1	2	3	4	5
	Asks questions to understand others' points of view	1	2	3	4	5
	Waits for others to complete thoughts and sentences before commenting or concluding	1	2	3	4	5
	Often asks "one more question"	1	2	3	4	5
	Shares relevant information with those who might benefit	1	2	3	4	5
	Communicates to management appropriately	1	2	3	4	5
Transparent Critical Thinking	Asks questions to help others understand	1	2	3	4	5
	Asks questions to gauge others' opinions and ideas	1	2	3	4	5
	Encourages everyone to participate in discussions, especially those who seem shy or hesitant	1	2	3	4	5
	Takes time to explain assumptions behind her conclusions	1	2	3	4	5
Crediting Others	Credits others' accomplishments to managers as well as to peers	1	2	3	4	5
	When crediting others, notes how the action helps others or the organization	1	2	3	4	5
Honest and Complete Criticism	Says what is right about an action as well as what could be changed	1	2	3	4	5
	Balances the importance of good and poor behaviors	1	2	3	4	5
	Helps others improve performance with criticism and feedback	1	2	3	4	5
Effective Conflict Resolution	Triangulates conflicts by placing them outside of the personalities of those involved	1	2	3	4	5
	Looks for middle ground in conflicts	1	2	3	4	5
	Allows few conflicts to escalate out of control	1	2	3	4	5
	Resolves conflict to achieve specific, desired results	1	2	3	4	5
	Describes those involved in conflicts as having good intentions	1	2	3	4	5
	Total Score					

WORKSHEET: ASSESS THE CUSTOMER-PURPOSED HIDDEN LEADER

Think of a specific member of your team who you suspect is a customer-purposed hidden leader. Then read the descriptions below. For each one, circle the number from 1 to 5 that reflects how often you see that person behaving in that way. The higher the ending number, the more likely you have a customer-purposed hidden leader. The online worksheet will calculate for you automatically.

bit.ly/194qQfk

	Observed Behavior	Frequency (1=Never, 5=Always)				
Shows Enthusiasm for the Work	Conveys excitement about getting work done	1	2	3	4	5
	Projects positive energy and enthusiasm	1	2	3	4	5
	Expresses confidence in the value provided to customers	1	2	3	4	5
	Goes the extra mile to deliver on client promises	1	2	3	4	5
Balances Skill Proficiency	Competent at the technical skills required for the job	1	2	3	4	5
	Communicates so customers understand and accept	1	2	3	4	5
	Asks for help when needed for technical or communication issues	1	2	3	4	5
Maintains a Sense of Urgency	Maintains momentum when addressing customer needs	1	2	3	4	5
	Highlights the consequences of not taking action in discussions	1	2	3	4	5
	Keeps customers informed about what is happening	1	2	3	4	5
Acts Like an Owner	Actively uses company strategies to guide workplace decisions	1	2	3	4	5
	Understands in depth how and why clients use products and services	1	2	3	4	5
	Takes responsibility for client outcomes	1	2	3	4	5
	Asks questions to understand the customer's point of view	1	2	3	4	5
Champions Change	Asks questions to understand a change initiative's impact on the customer	1	2	3	4	5
	Asks questions to understand colleagues' concerns about change initiatives and ideas	1	2	3	4	5
	Helps others understand and accept the importance of and reasons for change	1	2	3	4	5
	TOTAL SCORE					

WORKSHEET: EVALUATE A HIDDEN LEADER

The better you can pinpoint a hidden leader's strengths, the easier it will be to develop missing skills and characteristics. Think of a specific person, and then review the pages that follow. Check the behaviors you have observed in all four areas: has integrity that shows, leads through relationships, focuses on results, and is customer purposed. The more checkmarks in each level, the more developed your hidden leader's abilities. The online worksheet will calculate this for you.

bit.ly/16Mu2hD

Notice that when you evaluate integrity that shows, you are evaluating both the hidden leader's ability to show integrity and others' perception of that integrity. There are no levels of integrity per se, because there are no variations on integrity. One has integrity or not. In terms of evaluating the hidden leader, then, you are simply evaluating that leader's ability to show the integrity that already exists within the leader's personality.

EVALUATE A HIDDEN LEADER: HAS INTEGRITY THAT SHOWS
Description: Has the courage to consistently adhere to a strong ethical code, even in difficult situations.

Behaviors of the hidden leader

Observed Behaviors	*Evaluate: Yes or No*
Carefully evaluates before making promises that will be hard to fulfill	
Keeps commitments regularly	
Matches actions to verbal commitments	
Informs colleagues regularly about changing workloads or deadlines	
Consistently adheres to a strong personal ethical code	
Acts in accordance with company values	
Addresses potential ethical issues before they become major problems	
Makes ethical decisions consistently	
Speaks up when integrity issues are on the table, even if they are unpopular	
Describes both sides of an issue or argument	
Confronts others who act unethically or dishonestly	

Behaviors of the hidden leader's colleagues

Observed Behaviors	*Evaluate: Yes or No*
Trusts the hidden leader to act in the best interests of the organization, its employees, and its customers	
Describes hidden leader's treatment of others as fair and honest	
Models personal ethical behavior on that of the hidden leader	
Identifies the hidden leader as a good resource to help resolve disputes, clarify ambiguous situations, and address challenges	
Describes support from the hidden leader for efforts, accomplishments, and professional development	

(Continued)

EVALUATE A HIDDEN LEADER: LEADS THROUGH RELATIONSHIPS
Description:

- Uses interpersonal skills effectively
- Exercises a sense of curiosity
- Values others
- Believes in personal value to others, whether as a co-worker or as a friend

Observed Behaviors

Level 1	Level 2	Level 3	Level 4
❏ Appears approachable and friendly ❏ Seeks the opinions of colleagues ❏ Actively develops new relationships across the organization ❏ Credits others privately for successes and contributions ❏ Communicates to supervisor appropriately concerning colleagues and work issues	❏ Establishes strong rapport with colleagues ❏ Works comfortably with colleagues to complete assignments ❏ Handles challenging situations without raising negative emotions in self, reducing conflict ❏ Demonstrates respect for others in public ❏ Gives honest and balanced feedback appropriately when asked ❏ Communicates to management appropriately concerning colleagues and work issues	❏ Asks questions to understand colleagues' issues and concerns ❏ Helps to manage conflict in his or her work group without raising negative emotions in others ❏ Helps others understand his or her thought process, making connections for listeners between important points ❏ Credits others publicly for successes and contributions ❏ Involves colleagues who appear shy or hesitant in discussions and conversations	❏ Promotes collaboration and teamwork throughout the company ❏ Manages conflict effectively at many levels throughout the company ❏ Connects with people in other teams or divisions that help improve results for the business ❏ Offers honest and balanced feedback appropriately ❏ Shares relevant information broadly throughout the organization

(Continued)

EVALUATE A HIDDEN LEADER: A FOCUS ON RESULTS

Description: Uses the ends to define the means to achieve a goal, and maintains independent initiative to act.

Observed Behaviors

Level 1	Level 2	Level 3	Level 4
❑ Maintains initiative to achieve assigned objectives ❑ Focuses actions on business priorities and goals ❑ Effectively addresses barriers to goals ❑ Expresses personal commitment to achieve assigned objectives	❑ Displays a sense of urgency for achieving goals ❑ Meets commitments to attain goals ❑ Suggests new ways to improve efficiency and productivity ❑ Ensures that goals describe outcomes rather than process or input ❑ Productive beyond routine assignments	❑ Asks questions to determine the best processes to achieve results ❑ Adjusts or stretches process steps to achieve goals ❑ Describes end goals in terms of results ❑ Identifies a variety of actions that will achieve a goal ❑ Sets effective priorities to meet business goals and customer needs	❑ Provides ideas and information that influence the goals of the business ❑ Suggests procedural improvements to achieve results for customers ❑ Describes critical measures that most affect the company's performance

(Continued)

EVALUATE A HIDDEN LEADER: IS CUSTOMER PURPOSED

Description: Sees the big picture of the company's value promise and acts in ways that enable that promise for the paying customer.

Observed Behaviors

Level 1	Level 2	Level 3	Level 4
❑ Shows authentic enthusiasm for the job	❑ Demonstrates passion for delivering value to the customer who pays	❑ Encourages others to link their work to the value promise of the organization	❑ Promotes loyalty to the organization based on its value promise and values
❑ Demonstrates adequate communication and technical job skills	❑ Demonstrates an equal balance of average communication and technical job skills	❑ Demonstrates a balance of above-average communication and technical skills	❑ Demonstrates an equal balance of exceptional communication and technical skills
❑ Asks for help when skills are inadequate or situations are challenging	❑ Asks for help when skills are inadequate or situations are challenging	❑ Cultivates customer relationships that provide insight into potential improvements	❑ Suggests ways to adapt company strategy to support customer expectations
❑ Describes how customers experience the organization	❑ Routinely interacts with customers to get feedback on business performance	❑ Uses customer data to influence business objectives	❑ Looks for ways to keep up with changes in the marketplace or customer base
❑ Describes the importance of making a difference for customers	❑ Displays a sense of urgency for achieving goals	❑ Prompts a sense of urgency in others to meet customer needs	❑ Promotes change initiatives by helping others commit to the change
❑ Responds rapidly to customer needs and concerns	❑ Helps others understand the need for major changes in process or market approach	❑ Supports change initiatives by integrating initiative goals into actions	
❑ Accepts change initiatives in performing job responsibilities			

WORKSHEET: EVALUATE YOUR COMPANY'S INTEGRITY

While most people believe they have integrity, their actions may indicate that their code of ethics is not strong or consistent, or they lack courage to speak truth during conflict or in difficult situations. The same is true of organizational cultures. How peers and executives respond to hidden leaders' visible integrity illustrates the company's level of integrity. Use the statements below to assess how well your company supports hidden leaders and their integrity. Access the worksheet online for an automatic score.

bit.ly/1gg382X

Statement	Frequency (1=Never, 5=Always)				
C-level executives stress the importance of integrity as part of their regular communications.	1	2	3	4	5
Your company's stated values reflect strong ethical concepts.	1	2	3	4	5
Actions by executives, managers, and supervisors consistently reflect the stated values of the organization.	1	2	3	4	5
When employees or peers point out ethical dilemmas, others listen and use the comments as the basis for discussion.	1	2	3	4	5
When employees question processes or actions based on their inconsistency with the company's values, employees are rewarded or commended by someone in management.	1	2	3	4	5
In ambiguous situations, the company's leaders refer to the stated values as a means of determining action.	1	2	3	4	5
People in general commend, reward, or mention employees who get excellent work done.	1	2	3	4	5
Managers and supervisors credit the people they manage for successful results.	1	2	3	4	5
Most people speak openly about issues and concerns.	1	2	3	4	5
People talk to each other about conflicts instead of going behind the scenes to get others to deal with the issue.	1	2	3	4	5
People who challenge the status quo remain with the organization for long periods of time.	1	2	3	4	5
Total Score (Higher score=More integrity)					

ASSESSMENT: YOUR ORGANIZATION'S CULTURE

How functional is your company's relational culture? This assessment will help you understand areas where your culture may be making success difficult. Read each of the statements and assign a value to each. The lower the score in each area, the more that area may be negatively affecting your organization's culture. The online worksheet calculates the assessment for you.

bit.ly/195kaf1

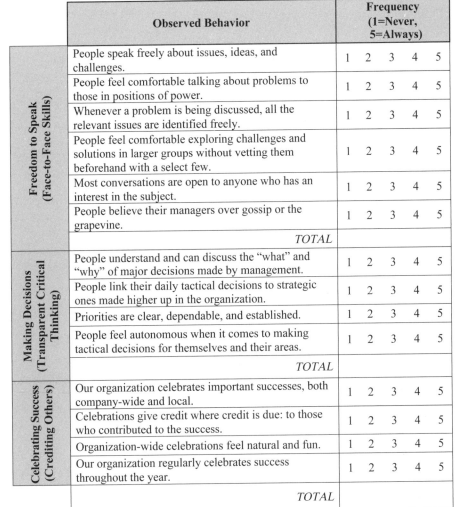

	Observed Behavior	Frequency (1=Never, 5=Always)				
Freedom to Speak (Face-to-Face Skills)	People speak freely about issues, ideas, and challenges.	1	2	3	4	5
	People feel comfortable talking about problems to those in positions of power.	1	2	3	4	5
	Whenever a problem is being discussed, all the relevant issues are identified freely.	1	2	3	4	5
	People feel comfortable exploring challenges and solutions in larger groups without vetting them beforehand with a select few.	1	2	3	4	5
	Most conversations are open to anyone who has an interest in the subject.	1	2	3	4	5
	People believe their managers over gossip or the grapevine.	1	2	3	4	5
	TOTAL					
Making Decisions (Transparent Critical Thinking)	People understand and can discuss the "what" and "why" of major decisions made by management.	1	2	3	4	5
	People link their daily tactical decisions to strategic ones made higher up in the organization.	1	2	3	4	5
	Priorities are clear, dependable, and established.	1	2	3	4	5
	People feel autonomous when it comes to making tactical decisions for themselves and their areas.	1	2	3	4	5
	TOTAL					
Celebrating Success (Crediting Others)	Our organization celebrates important successes, both company-wide and local.	1	2	3	4	5
	Celebrations give credit where credit is due: to those who contributed to the success.	1	2	3	4	5
	Organization-wide celebrations feel natural and fun.	1	2	3	4	5
	Our organization regularly celebrates success throughout the year.	1	2	3	4	5
	TOTAL					

(Continued)

	Observed Behavior	Frequency (1=Never, 5=Consistently)				
Addressing Failures (Honest And Complete Criticism)	Management uses failures as a means of learning how to succeed next time.	1	2	3	4	5
	People who fail while attempting to innovate are not punished but commended for the effort.	1	2	3	4	5
	To support success, managers give people the time, resources, and direction they need.	1	2	3	4	5
	Major failures are seen as the responsibility of many, not one person.	1	2	3	4	5
	New ideas and innovations are tested in front of many in the organization, not secretly.	1	2	3	4	5
	TOTAL					
Creative Conflict (Effective Conflict Resolution)	Conflicts are about ideas, solutions, challenges, and innovations—not personalities.	1	2	3	4	5
	People stay engaged when conflict arises.	1	2	3	4	5
	Conflicts are resolved in "public": within the groups or teams where the conflicts arise.	1	2	3	4	5
	Conversations about conflicts are calm, rational, and focused.	1	2	3	4	5
	People voice opinions because they are not afraid of conflict.	1	2	3	4	5
	TOTAL					

ASSESSMENT: EVALUATE YOUR PERFORMANCE-MEASUREMENT SYSTEM

This assessment can help you evaluate your company's performance-measurement system. It will provide an overall picture of your system's status and identify potential directions for improvement. The higher the score, the more effective your system. The online worksheet will calculate this for you.

bit.ly/1e2aDZ3

Statements	Frequency (1=Never, 5=Always)
My personal performance-measurement goals are important to me and my organization.	1 2 3 4 5
I look forward to performance-measurement discussions and events.	1 2 3 4 5
Performance evaluations happen regularly, not just annually.	1 2 3 4 5
I clearly see the links between my goals and the company's vision, strategy, and goals.	1 2 3 4 5
In general, our performance measures are good yardsticks that do not cause unrelated challenges.	1 2 3 4 5
I regularly refer to my performance goals as a map to improving my performance on the job.	1 2 3 4 5
My performance targets help me determine the best way to get results.	1 2 3 4 5
I can meet all my performance targets without compromising what I consider to be my integrity or ethical considerations.	1 2 3 4 5
I can discuss how my performance goals help our customers.	1 2 3 4 5
Our performance measures reflect some of the important skills of hidden leaders.	1 2 3 4 5
My goals include qualitative and quantitative measurement criteria.	1 2 3 4 5
I can clearly state my organization's vision, strategy, and goals, especially in regard to the value promise to our customers.	1 2 3 4 5
I know that if I take initiative to accomplish something out of the ordinary, I will be commended even if I don't reach the goal the first time.	1 2 3 4 5
When my manager rewards me for my accomplishments, she provides something that is important to me personally.	1 2 3 4 5
TOTAL SCORE	

Notes

Chapter 2: *Identify Hidden Leaders*

1. Anne Murphy Paul, *The Cult of Personality Testing* (New York: Free Press, 2005), xiii.

Chapter 3: *Enable Integrity*

1. Rosabeth Moss Kanter, "Four Reasons Any Action Is Better than None," *HBR Blog Network*, March 28, 2011, accessed September 2013, http://blogs.hbr.org/2011/03/four-reasons-any-action-is-bet/.

2. Darcia Narvaez and Daniel K. Lapsley, "Moral Identity, Moral Functioning, and the Development of Moral Character," in Daniel M. Bartels, Christopher W. Bauman, Linda J. Skitka, and Douglas L. Medin, eds., *The Psychology of Learning and Motivation*, Vol. 50 (Burlington, MA: Academic Press, 2009), 249–252, accessed September 2013 at www3.nd.edu/~dnarvaez/documents/NarvaezLapsleyLearningMotivation.pdf.

Chapter 4: *Build Essential Relational Skills*

1. John H. (Jack) Zenger, Joseph R. Folkman, and Scott Edinger, *The Inspiring Leader: Unlocking the Secrets of How Extraordinary Leaders Motivate* (New York: McGraw-Hill, 2009), 47,47.

2. Scott K. Edinger, "Three Ways Leaders Make Emotional Connections," (Oct 10, 2012), *Harvard Business Review*, HBR.org.

3. Leo Tolstoy, *Anna Karenina*, trans. Richard Pevear and Larissa Volokhonsky (New York: Penguin Classics, 2004), 1.

4. Neil Rackham, "The Coaching Controversy," adapted from *Training and Development Journal*, v33 n11 (November 1979), 12–16, accessed June 2014 at http://www.ascenticg.com/hw_survey/hw.htm.

Chapter 5: *Create a Focus on Results*

1. George Santayana, *Life of Reason,* Vol. 1 (New York: Charles Scribner's Sons, 1905), 13.

2. Teresa Amabile and Steven Kramer, "Do Happier People Work Harder?," *New York Times* Sunday Review, September 3, 2011, accessed September 2013, http://www.nytimes.com/2011/09/04/opinion/sunday/do-happier-people-work-harder.html?_r=0.

3. Nikki Blacksmith and Jim Harter, "Majority of American Workers Not Engaged in Their Jobs," Gallup Well-Being poll, October 28, 2011, accessed September 1, 2013, http://www.gallup.com/poll/150383/majority-american-workers-not-engaged-jobs.aspx%20January.

4. Martin E. P. Seligman, *Authentic Happiness: Using the New Positive Psychology to Realize Your Potential for Lasting Fulfillment* (New York: Free Press, 2002), 100–104.

Chapter 6: *Instill Customer Purpose*

1. Steve Lohr, "Can Apple Find More Hits Without Its Tastemaker?" *New York Times,* January 18, 2011, accessed September 2013 at http://www.nytimes.com/2011/01/19/technology/companies/19innovate.html?_r=0.

2. Heather Boushey and Sarah Jane Glynn, "There Are Significant Business Costs to Replacing Employees," Center for American Progress, November 16, 2012, 1, 2, accessed September 2013 at http://www.americanprogress.org/wp-content/uploads/2012/11/CostofTurnover.pdf.

3. Stefan Stern, "The Importance of Creating and Keeping a Customer," *Financial Times Limited* (October 10, 2011), accessed November 2013 at http://www.ft.com/cms/s/2/88803a36-f108-11e0-b56f-00144feab49a.html#axzz350x8MwrK.

Chapter 7: *Measure Performance*

1. Neil Rackham, conversation with Scott Edinger. Also described in "Putting That Smile Back Into Smile Sheets," *Training* (online edition), August 25, 2006, accessed September 2013 at http://www.cttnewsletter.com/article/putting-smile-back-smile-sheets.

Chapter 8: *Engaging Hidden Leaders*

1. Valve Corporation, *Valve Handbook for New Employees* (Bellevue, WA: Valve Corporation, 2012), 5, accessed September 2013 at http://www.valvesoftware .com/company/Valve_Handbook_LowRes.pdf.

Bibliography

Much of *The Hidden Leader* emerged from our combined many decades of work with companies and corporations of various sizes and in multiple industries. This partial bibliography encapsulates some of the books that have had the most influence on us during our careers.

Amabile, Teresa, and Steven Kramer. *The Progress Principle: Using Small Wins to Ignite Joy, Engagement, and Creativity at Work.* Boston: Harvard Business Review Press, 2011.

Covey, Stephen M. R., and Rebecca R Merrill. *The Speed of Trust: The One Thing That Changes Everything.* New York: Free Press, 2008.

Gabor, Andrea. *The Capitalist Philosophers: The Geniuses of Modern Business, Their Lives, Times, and Ideas.* New York: John Wiley & Sons, 2000.

Johnson, Steven. *Where Good Ideas Come From.* New York: Riverhead, 2010.

Kouzes, James M., and Barry Z. Posner. *Credibility: How Leaders Gain and Lose It, Why People Demand It.* Hoboken, NJ: Jossey Bass, 1993.

Loehr, Jim, and Tony Schwartz. *The Power of Full Engagement: Managing Energy, Not Time, Is the Key to High Performance and Personal Renewal.* New York: Free Press, 2003.

Paul, Anne Murphy. *The Cult of Personality Testing.* New York: Free Press, 2005.

Rackham, Neil, and Richard Ruff. *Managing Major Sales: Practical Strategies for Improving Sales Effectiveness.* New York: Harper Business, 1991.

Rifkin, Jeremy. *The Third Industrial Revolution*. New York: Palgrave Macmillan, 2011.

Santayana, George. *Life of Reason*, Vol. 1. New York: Charles Scribner's Sons, 1905.

Seligman, Martin E. P. *Authentic Happiness: Using the New Positive Psychology to Realize Your Potential for Lasting Fulfillment*. New York: Free Press, 2002.

Senge, Peter. *The Fifth Discipline: The Art and Practice of the Learning Organization*. New York: Doubleday, 2006.

Tolstoy, Leo. *Anna Karenina*. Translated by Richard Pevear and Larissa Volokhonsky. New York: Penguin Classics, 2004.

Valve Handbook for New Employees. Bellevue, WA: Valve Corporation, 2012. Accessed September 2013, http://www.valvesoftware.com/company/Valve_Handbook_LowRes.pdf.

Weiss, Alan. *Our Emperors Have No Clothes*. Pompton Plains, NJ: Career Press, 1995.

Zenger, John H., Joseph R. Folkman, and Scott K. Edinger. *The Inspiring Leader*. New York: McGraw-Hill, 2009.

Index

About the Authors

SCOTT EDINGER

Companies like AT&T, Lenovo, and the *Los Angeles Times* hire Scott Edinger to work with their senior leaders. Scott is recognized as an expert in helping organizations achieve measurable business results. He is coauthor of *The Inspiring Leader* (McGraw-Hill, 2009) and the *Harvard Business Review* article "Making Yourself Indispensable," called by the *Review* a "classic in the making." He is also a contributing author to *The American Society for Training and Development Leadership Handbook* (Berrett-Koehler & ASTD Press, 2010.) Scott has written dozens of other articles and white papers, and blogs for *Forbes* and the *Harvard Business Review*.

Scott has had the privilege of working with leaders in nearly every industry sector, helping them formulate and implement growth strategies, develop leadership capacity, increase revenue and profit, and attract and retain talent.

Prior to starting his firm, the Edinger Consulting Group, Scott was executive vice president for leadership consultancy Zenger | Folkman. In that role, he led the company to double in size. As senior vice president of sales for sales consultancy Huthwaite, he helped the firm achieve record levels of growth and success. Scott began his career at then–Big Six consulting firm Coopers & Lybrand (now PricewaterhouseCoopers.)

Scott resides in Tampa, Florida, with his wife, Christine, and their family.

LAURIE SAIN

A professional writer and instructional designer, Laurie Sain has defined content and created learning models for nearly five hundred thousand professionals, frontline supervisors, and workers. Her clients have included Apple, the Union Pacific, Fidelity Investments, and Charles Schwab, as well as some of the top training-consulting firms in the world. She is a specialist in developing programs to teach skills in sales, customer service, leadership, management, conflict resolution, and communication that are easy to learn, remember, and use. Tom Peters and other leadership gurus rely on Laurie to transform their books into effective training experiences. She is also a former contract editor for the *Harvard Business Review.*

As an interactive e-learning designer, Laurie has a deep understanding of the user experience of any product, whether it's as simple as a book or as complex as an online learning program. Hallmarks of her expertise are her tools, worksheets, and troubleshooting guides that employ simple approaches to help users gain major insights. Her clients say her ability to understand complex subjects and present them simply in clear, straight-forward language helps learners grow effectively in the shortest amount of time. Her philosophy that most skills and knowledge can be learned while working helps her create no-nonsense, productive, entertaining tools. Doing so allows the learner to simultaneously acquire new skills and get real work done.

Laurie is also a professional editor, presently editor in chief of *The Orff Echo,* the association quarterly of the American Orff Schulwerk Association, which promotes an interactive approach to teaching children music.

Laurie lives in Lander, Wyoming, with her husband, Craig Bromley, two cats, and a horse. After hours, she is a dedicated horsewoman and dressage rider and occasionally paints for pleasure.